C000063214

# The sociocultural and intercultural dimension of language learning and teaching

edited by

**Michel Byram**
*University of Durham, United Kingdom*

and

**Geneviève Zarate**
*Ecole Normale Supérieure de Fontenay/Saint-Cloud, France*

Education Committee
Council for Cultural Co-operation

Council of Europe Publishing

French edition:

*La dimension socio-culturelle et interculturelle de l'apprentissage et de l'enseignement des langues*

ISBN 92-871-3257-7

Council of Europe Publishing
F-67075 Strasbourg Cedex

ISBN 92-871-3256-9
© Council of Europe, 1997
Printed in Germany

# TABLE OF CONTENTS

# PREFACE

When launching the Council of Europe Modern Languages Project: *'Language Learning for European Citizenship'* the Education Committee identified a number of educational sectors and themes for priority treatment. In the course of the Project, which was conducted between 1989 and 1996, work in these areas was intensively pursued, partly by studies commissioned from leading experts in the field, but mainly in a series of 'new-style' workshops, attended by colleagues professionally active in the fields concerned. These were nominated by member governments and worked together under the leadership of 'animators' selected by the Council of Europe from among the acknowledged leading experts in Europe.

A 'new-style' workshop was held on the initiative of two co-operating member countries to deal with a theme identified by them as of particular importance. Each 'new-style' workshop had three phases. First, an initiating workshop of some five days' duration was held on the invitation of one member government. Here the aim was to establish the 'state of the art' in the sector or with regard to the theme, to identify areas in which further research and development work was needed, and then to set up an 'action programme' of projects to be carried out by individuals or institutions in two or more member countries under a project co-ordinator. In a second phase, this action programme was then conducted, normally over a two-year period, during which two Progress Reports on the conduct of the Projects were published. In a third phase, the outcomes of the Projects were reported by the Co-ordinators to a follow-up workshop, hosted by the second co-operating member government. Following the discussion of the projects and their products, the workshop concluded by setting out conclusions and recommendations regarding the general development of the field and future policy orientations.

Many of the new-style workshops have dealt with more than one priority sector or theme, and some themes to which a number of governments attached importance were the subjects of a number of workshops. As a result, contributions relating to particular priority sectors and themes were spread over a number of workshop reports, progress reports and independent studies. In addition, constraints on workshop time and report space have placed strict limits on the animators' introductions to workshop themes. The Council of Europe has therefore decided to commission a series of Compendia, each of which would bring together a number of the more significant contributions made to the Project in respect of one of its major areas of concern. In a number of cases this meant leaving aside a number of valuable contributions for which room could not be found in the agreed format, especially since authors have been given the opportunity to develop and up-date their contributions.

As the communicative approach to language learning and teaching has matured and the importance of mutual understanding and acceptance among Europeans has become more clearly recognised, we have come increasingly to realise not only that language is much more than a formal symbolic system for expressing ideas, but also that it is more than a means for carrying out practical transactions in every day life. It is also a powerful means for integrating the individual into a community and giving the community coherence and identity. As members of a community we learn in the course of our socialisation its rules and conventions concerning "who says what to whom, how, when and where" (Del Hymes). Inter-ethnic misunderstandings frequently arise as a result of an incompatibility between the conventions used by the partners, and between the systems of thought, values and beliefs which underlie them. For these reasons the development of a language learner's sociocultural competence with regard to the community or communities whose language he or she is studying has been seen to be of great importance. Michael Byram and Geneviève Zarate have played a very significant part in raising awareness of this dimension of language learning and in research into its better understanding, developing the concept of 'interculturality' as an educational objective. Using a foreign language in a way which shows understanding of its sociocultural dimension does not mean abandoning one's own cultural identity in order to become a carbon copy of native speakers, but rather developing a more complex personality in which both cultures interact, enabling the learner to bridge the cultural gap.

The sociocultural component in language learning has been one of the major concerns of the Project and we trust that the papers brought together here will help to strengthen this hitherto neglected aspect of language teaching.

*J.L.M. TRIM, Project Director*

# INTRODUCTION

*Geneviève ZARATE, France*

## Cultural issues in a changing Europe

### *Openness to democracy*

A number of major political events occurred during the period in which the Council of Europe's new-style workshops were held. The concept of Europe was altered considerably:

- Firstly, the European Community established a multilateral treaty for which each country voted, the Treaty of Maastricht. From being a Community, it became a Union. From being an abstract entity, Europe became the subject of a discussion in which every citizen was invited to take part. Europe as an entity is now part of everyday life (passports, food purchases, travel, means of communication, university studies and so on).

- Secondly, the European Union was expanded: the Twelve became the Fifteen. To interpret that transformation as a mere increase in size would be to underestimate its impact: new cultural areas were added, Northern Europe is now well-represented and the number of lesser-used languages has increased.

- Lastly, Europe simultaneously and paradoxically became an unspecified political configuration: since the fall of the Berlin Wall, defining Europe has become a matter of variable geometry. The Council of Europe led the way in reflecting these developments by accepting new member states. The "Europe" conjured up in everyday usage, by the media, in schools and by politicians is sometimes a geographical Europe stretching from the Atlantic to the Urals, and sometimes a Europe whose boundaries are strictly confined to the fifteen European Union countries, but which accommodates special relations with former colonies and countries awaiting recognition (Turkey, Morocco and the former eastern bloc) and has geopolitical dimensions (Europe and the Mediterranean area, for example).

That image, at once precise and blurred, is not without repercussions when Europe sets itself the educational goal of affirming its identity. The approach chosen by the Council of Europe - the relationship between citizenship and modern languages - is political and legal (owing to the use of the concept of citizenship) and linguistic. The democratic ideal governs that choice and is reflected at the linguistic level (all the European languages are, in principle, on an equal footing) and at the cultural level (national culture is a matter in which each state has unfettered discretion).

It is important to stress the direct social and cultural impact of the events which took place during the programme period. New states' accession to the Council of Europe altered the way in which participants were recruited for the workshops: teachers from the former east European countries joined the programme.

The Council of Europe has played a role in the developments in central and eastern Europe through the activities of the European Centre for Modern Languages and the specific activities of the Modern Languages Section. However, the fact that those countries took part in the workshops, which was not foreseen initially, did not modify the workshop format. Nonetheless, if we accept that language teaching and learning are connected with identity-based content, their participation gives rise to the following issues in the field under consideration in this collection:

- given that the new member states of the Council of Europe were previously separated from the founding countries by what was commonly known as the "iron curtain", their arrival reflects an ideological transformation which is one of the major events of this century;

- given that democracy is the cement of European identity, the entry of countries whose very titles previously contained the term "democratic", albeit with different meanings and different social and cultural practices, means that history and the way it is learned in schools are of vital importance;

- the inclusion of new cultural areas (Nordic, Slav and Austro-Hungarian) has given rise to broader diversity than that contained in the states which formed Europe's original core; the concept of diversity has consequently become more complex.

These aspects were not specifically addressed by the new-style workshops, but did have an impact on them. For all the participants, the workshops were an opportunity for previously unheard-of contact between representatives of countries which had been virtually closed to one another, and with thought patterns which had been learned in ideological environments based on radical opposition and institutionalised hostility (the Cold War). Different teaching practices crossed paths; for instance, there was the question of the commercial publication of school textbooks as opposed to state textbooks, and the question of whether language teaching could or could not be combined with travel abroad. When cultural difference was not the subject of organised discussion, it was the workshops' blind spot, but it was highlighted in the working documents and was part of the participants' experience.

*Education as a means of fostering openness to others*

The concept of openness to others is frequently put forward as a justification for learning foreign languages. It is used as much by politicians as by educationalists, and is very convenient. It is consensual: who could advocate *closure to others*? It is a concept that is easy to use owing to its semantic fluidity: does it mean promoting the learning of a language which has recently been introduced into an education system? Does it mean encouraging educational partnership between European regions in which the languages of both partners are identified as instrumental? Or does it mean justifying the impact of the constraints of a European policy on a given country? These arguments, like others which might also be mentioned, are disparate and do not embrace an underlying concept capable of justifying educational choices based on a theoretical connection. Arguments in favour of language learning in the name of openness toward other countries, which may be found in political approaches to education, tend to mask the weak theoretical bases on which those approaches operate.

Assessment of modern language skills is generally specific to each state, whether as part of a national policy or a private system. Citizens' need for mobility in their daily lives leads to a search for common assessment procedures in countries wishing to intensify their economic and cultural relations. The European ideology governing the formulation of an educational strategy is based on the following points:

- genuine democracy is affirmed in identity-based terms according to the model of parity between the national cultures present in the European political arena;

- European citizenship, an affirmation of political unity, is expressed in educational terms as the tolerant affirmation of national differences;

- for the European Union countries, the principle of subsidiarity entails "bringing the common cultural heritage to the fore" (Article 128 of the Treaty);

- geographical mobility within Europe encourages people to gain experience of other countries, beyond national frontiers.

How can that political desire be translated into practice? If an assessment and certification project based on international coherence is set up in the next decade, it will doubtless be necessary to produce a didactic model for assessing the cultural component in language learning. This approach precludes definitions associated with strict promotion of a given country's prominent national values, anchored in a logic of competition between languages, and encourages people to dissociate the cultural component from approaches which may result in nationalist excesses.


## Sociocultural/intercultural dimension: questions of definition

*Methodological problems*

Relative agreement has been reached on questions of method among trainers concerned about the intercultural dimension:

- The dichotomy between learned culture (legitimated culture, academic culture) and culture in the anthropological sense (referring to a description of everyday events) has become mundane among trainers who have received specific training in this field. Literature and history teachers are those most directly involved in incorporating an awareness of anthropological issues into their teaching: this focus on everyday life is generally demonstrated in the choice of teaching aids.

-   The concern to incorporate the concept of linguistic and cultural diversity into the description of cultural realities is also well established. Linguistic diversity criteria remain a delicate issue for learners, who must be convinced of the effectiveness of the teaching they receive in the standard language. Social and regional diversity and gender criteria are closely linked to national traditions: certain countries, such as the Scandinavian countries, are sensitive to such issues; others consider that their inclusion might break school taboos. Differences between generations are generally present when the description is based on the family model. However, they tend to be diminished when the learner's age group is taken as a basis: in that case, the predominant standards and values are those shared by native speakers of the learner's own age, and the learner is invited to identify with them. Nonetheless, this concern for a minimum level of diversity is not in itself sufficient to make the conception of a national culture (German culture, for example) or that associated with a broad geographical area (Latin American culture) inappropriate. Generalisation and simplification are widespread precisely because of this *de facto* across-the-board approach.

Are these methodological reflexes an adequate explanation of an issue which is specific to language teaching? It is possible to identify three drawbacks which explain the methodological difficulties encountered in trying to establish a theoretical basis:

-   The first ensues from the very name of the field concerned. The expression "sociocultural" imposes a bifocal view of the issues in question. In a training situation, this leads to clashes which are not based upon solid conceptual reflection: The difference between Mr Byram's and Mr Dahmen's approach is that Mr Byram prefers to speak about cultural competence, whereas Mr Dahmen pointed out several ways in which students gradually attain social-cultural competence by developing social skills (Report on Workshop 1A, Doc. CC-Lang (91) Workshop 1A: 64). Participants tend to base their ideas on subject divisions, defined generically, rather than using concepts that are valid because of their cross-disciplinary relevance and ensuing weight.

-   The second drawback results from the cultural policies for the dissemination of each national language beyond the country's frontiers. Such policies are specific to each country. They are based both on the nation's awareness of the past and on the cultural influence that they are intended to have internationally. If we take up the analyses proposed by Norbert Elias in his chapter on the formation of the "culture"/"civilisation" antithesis in Germany in *"Über den Prozess der Zivilisation"* (1st new edition, 1939), the term *Kultur*, used to explain the specific nature of the German soul, refers to the intellectual output and particular features of groups in a nation which is anxiously questioning the foundations of its national identity. The English and French use of the term *civilisation* is completely different. The term goes back to unquestioned confidence in an ideal of Progress and Humanism which France identified, in the colonial period, with Reason, Human Rights and the city. These countries' expansionist vision is justified by the universalism of their values. These traditions, which are at the core of each country's national identity, explain the profound differences in the way they view the dissemination of their values beyond their frontiers.

- Thirdly, although it is impossible to establish a clear correlation between the preceding observations and those which follow, it should also be noted that the university traditions in western Europe in the field described here are very varied. *Landeskunde, Cultural studies* and *Area studies* are terms which have grown out of different educational pasts. Subject divisions (history and literature, for example) do not necessarily correspond to geographic divisions. The latter may result in an extremist view of the cultural influence of a given language in a logic of implicit international competition. Staffing constraints (juggling the different skills available among teachers in a particular department) can sometimes be detrimental to conceptual coherence (this is sometimes the price to be paid for the introduction to "cultural anthropology" which is included in the initial training of teachers of French as a foreign language in French universities). Without arguing for intellectual standardisation, which is inconceivable in any case in the social sciences, in the broad sense of the term, we would point out that methodological reflection, although discussed in certain higher education disciplines (psychology, sociology, demography and anthropology), only has a very vague influence on the structure of such university subjects when they are defined according to a single logic, whether national, linguistic or geographic.

## The intercultural dimension: definition, objectives and evaluation

### The intercultural speaker model

In what follows, three features distinguish our approach from the more common ones:

- Firstly, the language learner is viewed as an intercultural speaker (as opposed to a native speaker). He or she is seen as somebody who crosses frontiers, and who is to some extent a specialist in the transit of cultural property and symbolic values. Rather than focusing on the concept of national territory which governs the traditional descriptions used to present a culture to somebody who is unfamiliar with it - particularly in educational contexts - our description focuses on the concept of frontiers. There is a rejection of metaphorical representations of a frontier as a line which can be crossed equally in one direction or the other. A particular kind of skill is therefore considered to be attached to the transmission of values between the native culture and the foreign culture being learned, and vice versa. It should be noted that the foreign culture/native culture relationship is often considered irrelevant in educational contexts, because it signifies the passage from the lesser known to the better known, or because it is assumed to be a symmetrical relationship and therefore equivalent to the native culture/foreign culture relationship.

The following objectives, for example, are closely linked to this definition of the learner as an intercultural speaker:

- the ability to identify areas of conflict in the relationship between two given communities;

- the ability to explain conflicting behaviour and beliefs;

11

- the ability to resolve conflict or to negotiate acceptance of unresolved conflict;

- the ability to evaluate the quality of an explanatory system and the ability to construct such a system on the basis of data from an interlocutor from a specific cultural background.

In the language learning context, geographic mobility is understood to engender a medium-length experience of the country whose language is being learned. This contrasts in particular with the tourist's experience - short and resulting in stereotyped contacts with the country visited - which was one of the models explored by the Council of Europe in devising a *"Threshold Level"*. It assumes a more demanding experience of cultural difference which takes account, for example of:

- the phenomena of resistance to discovering an unknown area without arrangements for assistance (as is the case in a commercial tourist experience);

- the length of time it takes for the learner to become integrated into a social community to which he or she does not belong;

- the approximative use of a language in crucial situations where failure to use it would result in rapid or serious social sanctions for the learner.

The following are examples of geographical mobility objectives:

- the ability to make and sustain personal contact with one or more members of the foreign community;

- the ability to identify the hallmarks of belonging to a socioprofessional environment;

- the ability to manage spatio-temporal constraints (for example, arriving punctually in an unknown place).

A number of skills are proposed in order to deal with the obvious issue of cultural difference. We have grouped them under the generic term "savoir-être" (life skills), which is defined as an affective capacity to relinquish ethnocentric attitudes towards and perceptions of others and a cognitive ability to establish and maintain a relationship between native cultures and foreign cultures. The associated affective and cognitive dimensions extend the language teacher's traditional role and invite him or her to take on new responsibilities, such as addressing ethnocentric attitudes, openness to others and reflection on the native culture, which may be activated by an experience of cultural difference.

The following examples illustrate this approach:

- knowing how to identify the ethnocentric effects of a document from the learner's own culture;

12

- the ability to identify situations in which different national values are enhanced or belittled (tourist's or colonist's approach);

- the ability to put one's own viewpoint and system of values in perspective in given situations.

### Evaluating intercultural skills

Whilst these examples can easily be related to a European ideology based on the concept of tolerance, it is noticeable that they are not quite so easily geared to the more controversial task of defining the relationship between different cultures. The social vision of this project is derived from the potential for conflict which always exists between two communities, the obstacles faced by "non-natives" entering a community which is not their own, and the notions of identity which go to make up people's perceptions of others and prompt them to look beyond their own immediate situation to think about the decisions which preside over medium-term expatriation.

For the sake of clarity, the range of examples of objectives has been divided into 4 main categories: existential competence (or "savoir-être"), the ability to learn (or "savoir-apprendre"), declarative knowledge (or "savoirs") and skills and know-how (or "savoir-faire"). When a curriculum is devised, different means of assessment are applied to each of these categories. Two criteria have been adopted to select the type of assessment for each category: some objectives are linked to a skill attached to a specific language whereas others are necessary regardless of the particular language involved. Furthermore, assessment often takes place at the end of a course of training - this is the most usual means of assessment - whereas for certain objectives assessment takes place at the beginning of the course.

Although skills linked to *savoir-être* are regarded as being independent of a specific foreign language, they may be developed only in the context of a particular language. This condition is intended to avoid the trap of a theoretical style of teaching either designed to be universal or made up of a range of geographically or nationally diversified cultural practices. However, although these skills are to be acquired in the context of a particular language, they are also supposed to be "transferable" to other cultural systems. By "transferable" we mean that skills acquired when learning one language can be applied again when learning another language. Therefore a different approach to learning will be taken depending on whether the language is the learner's first foreign language or his/her second one.

*Savoir-apprendre* involves the ability to devise and implement an interpretative strategy which sheds light on unfamiliar cultural meanings, beliefs and practices associated with a language or a culture with which the learner may or not be familiar. Although this skill is seen as independent of the learning of a given foreign language, it does result from learning one or more foreign languages. Assessment is conclusive in nature and measures abilities which can be transferred to other unknown languages and cultures. Therefore assessment must confront learners with unknown cultural practices and present them with situations in relation to which they must show their degree of understanding.

*Savoirs* represent the aspect which is present in the traditional notion of cultural references. They are defined as a system of cultural references which structures implicit and explicit knowledge acquired in the course of linguistic and cultural learning, taking into account the specific needs of learners in their interaction with speakers of the foreign language. This type of skill depends on the learning of a given language and a given context of use. It is assessed initially at the beginning of a course of learning because it may be impossible to supply a complete list of knowledge constituting the entirety of a culture.

The term *savoir-faire* refers to an ability to combine the three aforementioned skills in specific situations of bi- or multicultural contact. It implies an ability to make appropriate use of academic knowledge within the intercultural confines of a non-educational setting; an ability to recognise any special links between the cultural identity of learners and those of their foreign counterparts, as members of a given society; an ability to relate the perceptions existing within the learner's culture to those expressed by target language speakers. This skill is basically a relational one and therefore depends on the learning of a given language and cannot be applied directly to the learning of another language since it is based on the specific nature of relations between two cultural systems.

# INNOVATIVE PRACTICES FROM "NEW-STYLE" WORKSHOPS

# THE INTERCULTURAL DIMENSION IN 'LANGUAGE LEARNING FOR EUROPEAN CITIZENSHIP'

*Michael BYRAM, United Kingdom*

In the current programme on 'Language Learning for European Citizenship', four sectors of education were identified to be the foci of workshops and associated research and development:

- early language learning, referring to the period before the start of secondary education, usually about age 11;
- upper secondary education, a stage which varies considerably in the age range involved from country to country, but roughly defined as age range 15/16 to 17/19;
- advanced adult education, defined as that which has objectives beyond those found in compulsory education;
- vocationally orientated education and training, i.e. that which combines preparation for work with continuing general education.

(*Transparency and Coherence in Language Learning in Europe: objectives, assessment and certification.* Report on the Ruschlikon Symposium, p.5)

A second level of focus was then determined and a number of themes decided which would be pursued within each sector:

- use of mass media and new technologies;
- bilingual education (the use of more than one language as a medium of instruction);
- integration of visits and exchanges (including distance exchanges) into the curriculum - la pédagogie des échanges;
- "learning to learn", the preparation of pupils and students for independent learning;
- appropriate and effective methods of assessing and evaluating both the proficiency of learners and the effectiveness of the teaching/learning process.

Insofar as one accepts the argument made earlier in this volume that language learning must have a cultural dimension, that competent intercultural speakers have particular skills and knowledge (the four *savoirs*), it would appear self-evident that language learning in each of the four sectors should include that cultural dimension. Two sectors require more detailed consideration, however, before we discuss the themes identified for each sector.

First, consider the issue of intercultural competence in early learning. Early language learning which takes place within a primary school environment does so simultaneously with a crucial process of secondary socialisation in which young children are learning, in direct and indirect ways, to be members of a particular society. The school curriculum, both overt and hidden, introduces them to the beliefs, values and behaviours

17

which a society establishes for its members. This includes developing a sense of place and time in which one lives, acquiring an awareness of one's own country and nationality, and also acquiring a concept of otherness through which foreign countries and societies are defined as contrasting with one's own. Research in developmental psychology (Wiegand, 1992; Barrett and Short, 1992) suggests that this process of definition of self and others in terms of country and nationality continues throughout the period when early language learning is being introduced. The question then arises whether the model of an intercultural speaker able to mediate between own and other cultures and cultural identities, can be used to describe what may or should be taking place, or indeed to set objectives for early language learning.

The second sector requiring further consideration is vocationally orientated language learning. The issue here is that a cultural dimension needs to include the specific reference to workplace cultures. In this case a successful intercultural speaker is one who can not only relate the beliefs, values and behaviours of their own and another society but also mediate between what might appear to be the same professional worlds which are in fact different in subtle but powerful ways. Language learning for the specific purposes of the workplace might suggest to the learner that they share a professional identity and culture with colleagues of another language and country, but similarities are often misleading as the literature on international commerce indicates (Seelye and Seelye-James, 1995).

Turning now to the themes identified for research and development, let us first consider at a level of general principle how the cultural dimension and the development of intercultural competence might be expected to appear in each theme.

*The specification of appropriate objectives and the assessment of proficiency*

It is clear that a specification of objectives to develop intercultural competence is crucial. What is difficult to determine is how those objectives can be precisely formulated and, more crucially, how this process can be related to proposals for assessment, as we suggested in the previous section. It is for this reason that we have put two themes together here. The first paper, by Ana Artal, Maria José Carrión and Gemma Monrós describes an attempt to do this and provides detailed material exemplifying the formulation of objectives and relating them to other types of objectives for upper secondary education. This was work done within the authors' responsibilities in their own education system but linked to research and development arising from Workshop 1A.

*The integration of visits and exchanges into the curriculum.*

The model of intercultural competence defined as four *savoirs* makes explicit both cognitive and affective aspects of learning. Moreover, in *savoir-apprendre*, we have defined a skill which is of particular relevance to learning and experience in a new cultural environment. Visits and exchanges which take learners 'into the field', as ethnographers would describe it, are the richest and most complex opportunity for learning which can be offered to learners in any of the prioritised sectors of education.

18

The total experience of another environment, provided pupils are well prepared and given the opportunity not only to experience but also reflect on that experience, is unlikely to be matched by classroom learning. 'Distance exchange' - interaction with specific, identified speakers of another language and culture by telematic means - is a significant addition to classroom learning and can be combined with a visit or exchange. Unfortunately this theme was taken up late in the programme (in Workshop 18). However, because we believe that visits and exchanges are one of the most important means of developing intercultural competence, we are very pleased to have a paper by Mitteregger which describes the training of teachers in the pedagogy of exchanges. This is based largely upon previous work carried out in Switzerland, and upon the development of networks of teacher trainers as a consequence of the Workshop. It is evident from this paper that teacher trainers need mutual support in their different countries and areas of expertise in this new area of pedagogy.

*Use of mass media and new technologies*

We have already suggested that telematics are potentially a significant development in the opportunities for putting learners in personal and direct contact with others in other cultures and societies. They bring a 'virtual reality' of that otherness into the experience teachers can structure for learners in the classroom. But this is a virtual reality inhabited by real people in other countries, not one invented by the computer. Daniela Sorani and Anna Rita Tamponi describe in their paper (from Workshop 14) how this can be done in practice. It is not simply another means of confronting learners with the latest information about another country and culture. It is a means of helping them to learn to engage with otherness, even though it may be distant in space. The advantage of telematics is that distance in time, the delays of exchanges of information by mail for example, can be overcome and thereby diminish the distance in space.

*Learning to learn*

*Savoir-apprendre*, we have already suggested, is crucial to intercultural competence. Roland Fischer takes a similar perspective, emphasising that the presentation of information is not an appropriate method for developing intercultural competence. Learners need to acquire ways of gathering their own information and, more importantly, placing phenomena within the parameters of another cultural system. He gives examples of techniques and their application based on work done in Workshop 14.

'Learning to learn' is clearly related to this perspective in its emphasis on developing in learners a potential to engage with the unknown in an independent way. Anne-Brit Fenner has been working on this principle for several years with a focus on equipping learners to acquire linguistic competence. In her paper in this volume she describes how she adapted her experience to the cultural dimension as a consequence of Workshop 13A. In doing so, she recognised a need to develop her teaching techniques in order to guide learners in their process of learning to learn about another culture, in ways which make the relationship of 'learning to learn' and *savoir-apprendre* explicit and clear.

The use of a foreign language as a medium for teaching the existing curriculum does not necessarily provide an opportunity for developing intercultural competence. For example, if the existing history curriculum is taught in a foreign language this does not necessarily lead to a new perspective which challenges the taken-for-granted reality into which learners are socialised by the process of education. Interpretations of history are notoriously nationally biased, as are geographical representations of the world. There is the danger that the foreign language is simply used to encode an existing interpretation of reality, at the risk of distorting the language to 'fit' the reality portrayed in the curriculum.

On the other hand, the potential for confronting and comparing different interpretations of 'the same' reality in different languages and cultures is particularly rich in bilingual education. Textbooks in learners' own language can be used alongside those of another language and culture to help learners to relativise both accounts, and to accept that both are needed, not that one is 'correct' and the other 'false'. This would be a very effective way of developing a sophisticated level of *savoir-être*, in particular its affective aspect.

This is, however, a dimension of bilingual education which does not appear to have been addressed during the Programme and we cannot yet refer to a project which might illustrate the issues in practice.

All of these different approaches to intercultural competence pre-suppose that teachers themselves have such competence and, just as importantly, have a meta-cognitive awareness of their competence. They are then able to reflect on the objectives they wish to achieve with learners and develop appropriate methods such as those described in this volume. It is thus fortunate that as a consequence of Workshop 13A, a research and development network was set up in Finland and one of its members Säde-Pirkko Nissilä decided to focus on initial teacher training. The article describes in some detail how a new element was introduced into a course for trainee teachers and gives an account of the effects, as reported by the trainees themselves.

In the following section, the reader will find the articles introduced above. Thereafter, we offer a summary and some conclusions which can be drawn from these case studies.

## References

Barrett, M. & Short, J. (1992) "Images of European people in a group of 5-10-year-old English schoolchildren". *British Journal of Developmental Psychology,* 10, pp. 339-63

Seelye, H.N. & Seelye-James, A. (1995) *Culture Clash.* Lincolnwood: NTC Business Books.

Wiegand, P. (1992) *Places in the Primary School.* London: Falmer Press.

# CAN A CULTURAL SYLLABUS BE INTEGRATED IN THE GENERAL LANGUAGE SYLLABUS?

*Ana ARTAL, Mª José CARRIÓN, Gema MONRÓS, Spain*

In the present article we present the theoretical approach and a practical implementation of the part of the Valencian Community Guidelines for the Foreign Languages Curriculum referring to sociocultural contents.

## Introduction

*Contextualisation of the curriculum renewal*

The general reform of education recently undertaken in Spain has brought a lot of changes. Among the most outstanding ones are the raising to 16 of the school leaving age, making secondary education compulsory and state supported, the updating of the curricula, and the design of teaching guidelines.

In the present political system, educational responsibilities in Spain are divided among different bodies: The Ministry of Education establishes a common curricular core for the whole country and then agrees with the Local Autonomous Councils the setting up of a differentiated part of the curricula for each area. Within these legal guidelines, the schools themselves and their different departments can make the final adaptations according to factors concerning the community where the school is situated and the needs and goals of the particular school; the result is the School Curriculum and the Syllabi of the different areas, which are supervised by the administration.

*Brief description of the rationale and the curriculum guidelines*

The new approaches for the renewal of the curricula are based on three main assumptions:

- sociological
- psychopedagogical
- epistemological

Among the sociological assumptions, the fact that Valencia is a bilingual community (Spanish and Catalan co-exist on different levels for historical, geographical and social reasons) and that two foreign languages can be learned at secondary and post-secondary levels, led the designers of the languages curricula to propose an integrated approach to the teaching of first, second and foreign languages. This decision is based on the notion that communicative competence is common and underlies the knowledge of one or several languages and therefore, this should be taken into consideration when developing each particular curriculum. This assumption is reinforced by psychopedagogical research which states that concepts acquired in the first language act as preconcepts for the learning of second and third languages.

From the epistemological point of view, a pragmatic theory of language has been adopted. This theory considers communicative ability as the sum of discourse, linguistic, sociocultural and strategic competences. As a result, the Foreign Language Curriculum in the Valencian Community has been organised in four main blocks of contents:

1. Communicative contents: language in use at receptive and productive levels. The aim is to establish interpersonal communication, process information from different sources and respond to the creative uses of language, according to sociocommunicative and cultural norms.

2. Language awareness contents: study of the system of language: phonology, morphology, syntax, textual aspects.

3. Learner autonomy contents: the development of learning to learn and communicative strategies integrated in the learning of the language itself.

4. Sociocultural contents: sociocultural values are inseparable from language and therefore inseparable from language learning. This block includes different cultural aspects both implicit in language or existing socially and the knowledge of which is necessary to understand the values language transmits. On the other hand, the knowledge of different cultures must lead to awareness of and reflection upon one's own culture.

## Designing of objectives and contents

We have mentioned before the global and integrated character of all the components of communicative ability even if they are described and analysed separately. In the same way, the four types of contents we have presented try to separate the teaching-learning contents of the FL to facilitate didactic decisions. This will allow us to refer specifically to the sociocultural contents without referring to the other contents. However we want to insist on the fact that, in a communicative perspective of teaching a language, the interrelation and interaction between all the contents is inevitable.

The same psychopedagogical, epistemological and sociological reasons which are the framework of the FL curriculum design help us to justify the special attention given to the sociocultural contents in the curriculum. Among the first, we find the principle which states that the acquisition of a language involves a way of perceiving reality and is at the same time conditioned by this perception. Language and perception of reality are, therefore, two different aspects of the same construct shared by a social group. To acquire a language it will be then necessary to be able to perceive and understand the representations of the reality its speakers share.

These reasons connect with the epistemological ones: on a linguistic level, the dichotomy language-culture is even less justifiable than on the pedagogical one. As Halliday (1975) states, ..."The linguistic system is part of the social system. Neither can be learnt without the other". Indeed, if we analyse the linguistic system from the point of view of its 'dimensions of use', the main functions for which language is needed, we see that the sociocultural aspects are present in all of them. The *interpersonal dimension*, which involves interaction (social relationship) among speakers, implies the knowledge and the use of a series of norms and conventions more or less implicit, which rule this interaction. Through the *transactional dimension*, which allows the processing of information, we transmit meanings and concepts which arise from a particular vision of the world. Finally, by means of the *aesthetic-ludic* function speakers respond to imaginative uses of language. (Clark, 1987)

Among the sociological reasons, the existence of several official languages in Spain, and, above all, Spanish and Catalan in the Valencian Community, make it absolutely necessary to make students aware of the richness of linguistic, cultural or ethnic variety. To know and value foreign cultures helps to overcome the barriers which an ethnocentric vision of reality may build. To this objective we could add the first recommendation of the 1983 Conference for European Co-operation (Trim, 1983), which mentions "la necessité de prendre en compte les aspects culturels et sociaux de l'apprentissage de langues, en particulier de briser les stéréotypes nationaux et d'aider les apprenants à franchir les frontières affectives nationales".

*Classification of objectives and contents*

A first classification of objectives allows us to contemplate two types of objectives:

a.  the general objectives, arising directly from the main goals stated by the Educational Authorities in order to achieve a solidary, compensating school.

b.  the specific objectives, which outline the pedagogical aspects which have to be developed to achieve such goals.

Among the former the official curricula (D.O.G.V. 6-4-92) state:

-   To value the help that the knowledge of foreign languages involves in order to communicate with people belonging to cultures different to ours in the different fields of human activity.

-   To appreciate the richness that different languages and cultures offer as a different way of encoding experience and of organising interpersonal relationships, developing interest and curiosity towards the multicultural world we live in.

-   To maintain a receptive attitude towards information coming from the culture transmitted by the FL and to use that information to reflect upon one's own culture.

-   To show a critical attitude to discover the sexist, racist and classist stereotypes that the language may transmit.

23

Among the latter, the specific objectives try to gather the aspects which are needed to achieve a development of the sociocultural competence in foreign languages, justified by current research (Benadava, 1982; Byram, 1990 and 1992; Zarate, 1983; Valdés, 1986; Leblanc et al., 1990). They refer to:

- Acquisition of knowledge, (either conceptual or factual).

- Awareness and use of strategies to locate, analyse and interpret sociocultural contents transmitted by the target language.

- Development of behaviour and attitudes which help intercultural communication.

The contents follow the rationale of the selected objectives as well as the educational goals and can be classified as follows:

a.   Referential: which we can call 'ways of life', coming from the anthropological conception of sociocultural aspects.

b.   Sociocommunicative norms.

c.   Crosscurricular, fulfilling broad educational aims, such as peace and health education, etc.

d.   Cultural implicits and connotations.

e.   Attitudes towards languages and cultures. Values.

f.   Procedures and strategies to analyse and deal with contents.

*A proposal of sociocultural objectives and contents*

The objectives and contents we now present try to be just an example of how they could appear according to the proposals and guidelines mentioned above. They are checklists which could serve as a starting point for a selection relevant for a particular school context. The list is not meant to be complete nor exhaustive and, in any case, it should be completed with more concrete elements rooted in the context in each school and the particular teaching situation. On the other hand, the order in which the items are presented does not imply any hierarchy or progression. The relevant decisions will be taken according to criteria dictated by the situation, and depending on each didactic project (see Table 2).

The objectives can be specified as follows:

Students should be able to:

1. acquire or enlarge the referential knowledge which makes it possible to interpret the communicative contents in texts (oral, written, iconic) to get near the 'minimal knowledge' shared by the community which speaks the language.

2. know and interpret the gestural and non verbal codes used by the speakers of the language.

3. know and use the sociocultural norms suitable to different communicative situations.

4. enlarge the capacity to identify the cultural implicits which are present in the texts produced by different cultural communities.

5. identify the 'world of connotations' which the members of a given cultural community share.

6. employ localisation, observation and analysis techniques of the connotations present in texts.

7. locate and consult complementary information sources to build sociocultural notions.

8. develop positive attitudes of curiosity, open mindness and understanding of the cultural facts related to the target language.

9. develop awareness about the subjectivity with which the foreign culture is seen and become aware of the stereotypes that one's own culture has built of the foreign one.

10. develop awareness of the relativity of cultural spaces and facts.

11. develop instruments for intercultural communication founded on respect for the other and the appreciation of difference.

As for the contents, we could use the following selection as an example:

a. Referential contents

a.1. Symbols of identity:
   - festivals, emblems, outstanding personalities, objects, representative signs;
   - newspapers, representative broadcasts and media with a notable public influence in the community;
   - important and meaningful geographic and historic referents; meaning and values they stand for (eg Alésia for the French Community)

25

a.2. Everyday ways of life:
- housing;
- housing and environment: rural world, villages, towns;
- family: family roles; functions and relationships;
- education and schools;
- work; young people's entrance to the working world;
- leisure;
- social networks: socialising at different age levels.

b. Sociocommunicative norms:

b.1. Norms and interaction:
- greetings;
- polite formulas;
- proxemic norms.

b.2. Gestures: values and meaning

b.3. Conversation management:
- beginning a conversation;
- turn taking, opening, holding and relinquishing;
- topic switching;
- etc.

c. Crosscurricular topics. Of an educational nature, these are prescribed by the National Curricula for all the areas. They include topics such as peace and health education, co-education, environmental education, consumerism.

d. Implicits, presuppositions and cultural connotations: to be treated as they appear in authentic texts (oral, written or iconic); the teaching approach will consider the conditions of production and reception under which texts have been conceived.

e. Attitudes and values:

e.1. Awareness of the social values given to the world which appear in the texts.

e.2. Location and acknowledgment in texts of the stereotypes generated by a community in the use of language.

e.3. Awareness and critical vision of one's own prejudices and stereotypes and representations with respect to the target language.

f. Procedures and techniques. These contents aim to provide pupils with the strategies needed to learn and work autonomously with the rest of the contents. They include aspects such as:

f.1. Communicative strategies to repair misunderstandings of a cultural nature.

f.2.    Techniques to find information and reference sources.

f.3.    Techniques to find and select sociocultural information.

f.4.    Techniques to carry out project work on sociocultural topics.

## Proposal of criteria for selecting and sequencing sociocultural contents

We have established that culture is always present in the background of 'language learning' as something indissociable from the language itself. Our intention is to introduce the 'cultural contents' in an integrated way into our general discourse oriented syllabus.

Decisions have been taken about what language to teach the students, and the three dimensions of use, interpersonal, transactional and aesthetic described in 2, provide some guarantee that a range of texts and contexts are going to be present in our syllabus but now we have also to take into account the way social and cultural meanings are introduced to them. First, we have to consider the sociocultural meanings that have to be made explicit and the ones that could be communicated in an implicit way. Then, we also have to think about the foreign sociocultural meanings that make the students reflect on both the target and their own native culture. Finally, and because we are talking here about educating adolescents, we have to face cultural factors such as gender, race, ideology... and take them into account too in order to build up in the students cross-cultural personalities for the future.

*Some prior considerations*

To select sociocultural contents we are aware of the difficulties we have to overcome:

a.   vast quantities of items to choose from;
b.   risk of falling into ethnocentrism when taking decisions on what to choose;
c.   making students avoid subjectivity in their appreciations;
d.   lack of tradition in models of progression to follow;

When dealing with the selection and sequence of contents for our proposal, we have identified some considerations, bearing those difficulties in mind, in order to get some kind of guide for taking decisions.

The first consideration has to do with the *nature* of the sociocultural contents themselves. Some of these are easier to specify than others. Ways of life, cross-curricular subjects could easily be presented as checklists to be covered in relation to language work. Strategies for cultural and literary understanding can be developed if some time is dedicated to focus on procedures to learn how to inference and give learners the ability to work out cultural and literary meanings by themselves. Attitudes are  more difficult to specify and assess but it is important to have them as signposts to direct the cultural syllabus.

The second consideration refers to the *context* in which the sociocultural contents have to be covered. We must consider here context in a very broad sense. From the political and social, whether international, national or even local, to the private context of the school itself (school projects, cross-curricular work..). Nor can we omit either the particular context created in the classroom as a very important resource. To take advantage of all the opportunities that the linguistic, situational and interactional work provide can give a valuable key to explore the cultural meanings encoded in the foreign discourse. Of equal importance can be the temporal context in which students move on along the syllabus such as celebrations, events, exchanges, which coincide with the school year. All these contextual aspects will influence the inclusion at a precise moment of some contents or others according to their relevance and meaningfulness.

*Criteria for selecting and sequencing*

It will be useful to draw some flexible criteria to guide the selection and sequence of sociocultural contents for the implementation of the syllabus. The criteria can only orient the decisions that teachers themselves will have to take in each particular context according to their own situation. This, even more than the general syllabus, has to be left to a final level of concretisation that broad institutional guidelines cannot and should not provide.

The criteria we have elaborated in order to guide the selection and sequence of sociocultural contents are described below. The numbers do not imply a strict order but, on the contrary, the four criteria should interact to take the final decisions for each grade or cycle of studies.

1.   Meaningfulness in each particular context.
2.   Closeness to the students' lives and experiences.
3.   Possibility of establishing connections with their own culture.
4.   Explicitness with which the contents appear in the texts.

According to these criteria the *topics* we have selected for the first years of the secondary education are the ones the students are more familiar with as, for example, the way youngsters live in the countries where the target language is spoken, what they do in their free time, the most important celebrations and the way people live them. That familiarity with the topics will facilitate the possibility of establishing connections with the way the students live them and so it will give opportunities to establish some kind of contrast analysis. As for the *sociocommunicative rules*, we will focus on the basic ones needed for a successful communicative exchange such as how to address somebody to whom you must show respect or somebody you don't know; how to start a conversation or how to finish it. At the same time, the texts chosen for these years of study will have *explicit cultural referents* and the sociocultural rules will be very clearly understood. The oral or written *instructions given in the didactic activities* will also help their interpretation by the students and act as a guide for their achievement.

For the last years of secondary education, the same topics will be further developed but other ones not so closely related with the vital experience of students will be included.

The sociocommunicative rules developed in this period will include more subtle forms of management of conversation which can be observed in foreign interactions, for recognition and further performance. At this level, the recognition and interpretation of implicit cultural contents will be encouraged (connotations, stereotypes etc.. that very often leave traces in texts such as 'reactions' of the speakers). Procedures for research and investigation of sociocultural contents that lead to specific projects will also have an important part in this last period of compulsory education.

## Assessment and Evaluation

If sociocultural contents are to be learned, they must also be assessed. The school situation seems to give the status of 'contents to be programmed' only to the contents which are not evaluated and assessed according to predetermined parameters and criteria. Nevertheless, the difficulties in designing criteria and tools for the evaluation of these contents seem to be greater than those we find when we consider the evaluation of the other components of communicative competence. Some of the reasons for this could be :

- A 'quantitative' evaluation assessing the knowledge of a series of facts and data is possible. As a matter of fact, as Zarate mentions, "La Compétence culturelle ne peut échapper à la constitution d'un savoir fermé, somme de connaissances qui constitue un accés obligé à la compréhension d'un système culturel particulier" (Zarate, 1983, p. 38). However, such an evaluation runs the risk of not being scientific: an appearance of system projected by an organisation of contents which may be arbitrary.

- The evaluation of attitudes, one of the most important types of contents in the sociocultural block, can hardly be the object of a summative evaluation. We can, at least, consider if it is fair to give a mark for the development of a greater or lesser empathy.

- A qualitative evaluation of knowledge, especially of the perceptive and connotative contents such as representations or stereotypes, requires complex tools, which are perhaps not easy to design, and which have not yet been sufficiently studied and produced.

## Requirements for the evaluation of sociocultural contents

In the existing literature on sociocultural contents, there is little about evaluation. Nonetheless, some authors already tackle this problem and offer some hints of solution.

Zarate (1990: 55) proposes a converging treatment of the quantitative and qualitative aspects of this competence, which would be given through recognising as valuable the notion of representation. This involves the use of evaluation tools allowing, for instance, the connection of the representations with the social groups which originate them. Thus, in a given situation, students find a range of possible answers; what we evaluate is their capacity to separate possible and impossible answers. According to Zarate, qualitative evaluation of the sociocultural competence presents the following constants: a collective dimension or self-assessment; a prospective nature (to know and anticipate the effects of teaching), but also a formative one (awareness of the evolution of one's own representations); a reflexive nature, which asks for an interpretation of the experiences from a distance.

Following Denise Lussier (Lussier, 1992), we propose an evaluation of the sociocultural competence which will be achieved when considering communicative competence as a whole, even if it takes into consideration specific aspects. These aspects, which can be classified in 'savoirs-faire' or behaviours of different taxonomic levels (to locate, re-use, analyse, infer), are observed through the use of linguistic capacities in communicative situations, assessed according to parameters and criteria such as awareness of verbal and non-verbal signs, or the use, if necessary, of the suitable means and resources to fill the information gaps (from compensating strategies to bibliographic consultation). From this point of view, it is the success or the failure to communicate which would permit assessment of the degree of mastery of the aspects relating to sociocultural competence.

*Tools*

From our point of view, different types of contents within the same sociocultural block would demand different treatments as far as evaluation is concerned.

The 'ways of life' contents can be planned and presented in contextualised texts in concrete receptive and productive ways; this makes possible, not only the acquisition of referential knowledge of a 'quantitative' nature, but also the 'qualitative' analysis of those referents and of the world of representations and connotations that knowledge involves. Afterwards, the use of multiple-choice or 'true-false' questionnaires, will allow us to assess the degree of acquisition of the contents, the capacity to locate and interpret the implicits and to recognise stereotypes.

As for the 'sociocommunicative norms', their acquisition will preferably be assessed through the use of observation worksheets for communicative activities such as role plays or simulations.

Attitudes, as well as cross curricular contents, will be assessed through observation/self-observation questionnaires before and after the development of the contents.

An outstanding tool which permits all types of assessment (initial, formative and summative), and helps learning at the same time, is project work. When carrying out a project on sociocultural contents, pupils use techniques for the research, analysis and treatment of contents. They use and contrast different information sources and they contextualise, compare and assess them. Its presentation before the class permits an analytic treatment and the comparison with their own reality; for the teacher it is a thorough and complete means of assessment.

At the present moment of research, we feel that to keep to these minor suggestions can permit the evaluation of sociocultural competence from a proper perspective. In the future and with the development of broader works and with experience, we feel that it will be possible to go deeper into these matters and reach more complete and satisfying approaches.

## A practical model for implementation

The curriculum guidelines provided for the design of the syllabus and all the criteria drawn to help and guide our decisions are flexible enough to allow the development of quite different geographical syllabi. The basic idea is to offer a framework that is open enough to give freedom of action to the different autonomous regions, to the different schools in each region and to the different teachers in the different groups. There are some minimal requirements compulsory throughout Spain but provided these are covered, the decisions taken to design a syllabus can lead to substantially different syllabi.

There is the possibility of designing a task-based syllabus, a discourse syllabus based on the selection of specific genres, a content-based syllabus. It is also feasible to design the first draft for a process syllabus, open to negotiation with the students and to the development of the teaching-learning activities. Within these different types of syllabi, we can choose sociocultural contents as the backbone of our syllabus. The label given to each of them (task, discourse, etc.) shows the main axis that gives coherence to the syllabus but all the types of contents mentioned earlier in this article must also be present.

We shall present below an example of a cultural syllabus developed following the general guidelines shown so far. It is a part of the discourse syllabus designed to be implemented in the school year 95-96 with a group of 16-year-old students taking French as a first foreign language. Table 1 shows the sociocultural contents planned to be covered for that year. We must remember that this block of contents is presented as an integrated whole with the other three blocks Table 2 presents the different contents of a Unit of work in which the axis of the Unit comes from the sociocultural block of contents and where we can see the integration just named.

Table 1: A selection of sociocultural contents for a school year at upper-secondary level.

| Contenus référentiels | Représentations . Connotations. Stéréotypes | Normes et conventions sociocomm. | Contenus transversaux | Attitudes |
|---|---|---|---|---|
| 1. La famille | | | | Ouverture d'esprit devant une réalité autre. |
| a. famille et mode de vie. | Le HLM. Le pavillon de banlieue. Une ferme bretonne | | | |
| • types de famille selon le lieu de résidence (famille en milieu urbain, famille en milieu rural.) | | | | Esprit critique pour évaluer la propre réalité. |
| ■ familles et revenus. Distribution du budget selon les groupes sociaux. | Les représentations de ce qu'est le "luxe" selon les groupes sociaux. | | | |
| ■ familles, groupes sociaux et types de logement (dans les villes, les banlieues, en milieu rural). | | | | |
| ■ familles, logements et équipements. | | | | |
| ■ les "objets fétiches" selon les groupes sociaux (la voiture, la tv, l'ordinateur). | Les connotations des différents modèles de voiture. | | | Esprit critique pour analyser les effets de la consommation. |
| b. famille, rôles sociaux et modes de relation. | | | | Esprit critique devant les stéréotypes générés par les groupes sociaux. |
| ■ répartition des fonctions dans les familles selon les groupes sociaux | | Caractéristiques d'un dialogue entre parents et enfants (une famille de professionnels aisés). Modes de relation. | | |
| ■ l'éducation des enfants. | Stéréotypes sexistes dans l'éducation des enfants. | | Coéducation. Éducation pour l'égalité des sexes. | |
| ■ les travaux ménagers. | | ■ prendre la parole | | |
| ■ le status des enfants dans la famille | Le stéréotype de l'adolescente. | ■ rétorquer. ■ gestes et mimiques. Leur signification et emploi. | | |

Table 1 (continued).

| Contenus référentiels | Représentations connotations, Stéréotypes | Normes et conventions sociocomm. | Contenus transversaux | Attitudes |
|---|---|---|---|---|
| 2. Les lieux où l'on habite. | Représentations : la grande ville, la petite ville. | Modes d'entrée en relation et appartenance sociale. | Éducation pour la paix et la solidarité : variété ethnique et respect de la différence dans les communautés pluriculturelles. | Reconnaissance de la variété de cultures à l'intérieur d'un même pays. |
| ■ La vie dans la grande ville : les habitants des quartiers Nord de Marseille ; les quartiers vus par leurs habitants ; la Cité du Soleil à Paris, Montparnasse. | | | | |
| ■ La vie dans une petite ville (Vannes). | Connotations : la vie dans une cité pour les membres de différents goupes sociaux. | Le "parler jeune". Les copains de la cité et les tours de parole. | | Appréciation de la richesse que suppose le contact multiculturel. |
| ■ Villes et décor urbain (plaques, panneaux, enseignes...) | | | | Ouverture d'esprit devant le fait de la différence ethnique et culturelle. |
| ■ La vie dans une communauté rurale. | | | | |
| ■ La participation à la vie sociale selon les communautés. | La conception de la qualité de vie selon les groupes sociaux | | | |
| ■ Services, infrastructure et qualité de vie selon les communautés. | | Tours de parole dans la langue formelle : une séance municipale dans une mancommunauté rurale. | | |
| ■ Quelques villes importantes des différentes communautés francophones : images de Montréal, Genève, Lyon, Bruxelles. | | | | |
| ■ Toponymie des pays francophones (La France et le Québec). | Comment les habitants des différents villes/ régions / pays imaginent-ils les autres. | | | |
| ■ Régions et langues régionales : carte linguistique de la France. | | | | |
| | Connotations des noms et réalité historique. | | | |

33

Table 1 (continued).

| Contenus referenciels | Représentations, Connotations, Stéréotypes | Normes et conventions Sociocomm. | Contenus transversaux | Attitudes |
|---|---|---|---|---|
| 3. Les jeunes et le temps libre.<br>■ Temps libre, éléments et réseaux relationnels : la musique, les sports. Autres activités préférées selon les groupes sociaux. | Quelques stéréotypes d'adolescents : les "tribus urbaines".<br><br>Signes de reconnaissance : vestimentaires ; façons de parler ; les préférences musicales. | | Éducation pour l'égalité et la solidarité : les différences de conception et de déroulement du temps libre selon les groupes sociaux et selon les types de communautés. | Ouverture d'esprit devant les réalités autres. Dépassement de certains préjugés et stéréotypes sociaux. |
| ■ Les lieux privilégiés de la socialisation des jeunes.<br>■ Moyens de communication pour les jeunes. Quelques revues : Phosphore. | | | | Appréciation de la possibilité d'enrichissement culturel et humain que peut supposetr le temps libre. |
| ■ Loisirs et infrastructure institutionnelle : l'exemple des Maisons des jeunes et de la culture (en France).<br>■ Familles et temps libre : les vacances.<br>■ Les vacances au long de l'année : le décalage.<br>■ Lieux préférés pour les vacances. | Connotations des "vacances".<br><br><br>Représentations des lieux préférés pour les vacances. "Le Sud", "La mer", L'Espagne. | Le dialogue argumentatif. Les gestes de la protestation et l'argumentation. Intonation argumentative. Expressions phatiques et négociation de signifiés. | | |
| ■ Les familles et la télé. | | | | |

34

Table 1 (continued).

| Contenus référentiels | Représentations, connotations, Stéréotypes | Normes et conventions sociocomm. | Contenus transversaux | Attitudes |
|---|---|---|---|---|
| 4. Les jeunes gens et le travail.<br>■ Le travail agricole<br>■ Le travail industriel<br>■ Les services<br>■ Les professions libérales<br>■ L'entrée au monde du travail : le premier emploi.<br>■ Type d'études et emploi. Les étudiants face au travail. Les études les plus valorisées devant l'entrée au monde du travail.<br>■ Distribution de la population active.<br>■ Le travail "marginal" : les "petits jobs" ; le travail "au noir".<br>■ Nouvelles prefessions, nouvelles entreprises : l'initiative des jeunes<br>■ Modes d'organisation du travail selon différentes professions. | Représentations de la notion de "Travail". Évolution du concepte<br><br>Les professions les plus valorisées.<br><br><br>Stéréotypes sexistes dans les représentations du travail et les professions : professions "masculines" et prof. "féminines". Être "son propre patron"<br><br>Quelques stéréotypes : le PDG, le cadre, le patron. | Conventions sociocommunicatives dans certains types de textes. Oraux : interviews (sélection pour un emploi ); enquêtes .Écrits : c.v. ; lettres de demande d'emploi.<br><br>Coéducation. Éducation pour l'égalité des sexes. | | Valorisation de l'importance de la formation initiale .<br><br>Attitude éveillée et critique face aux différences générées par les préjugés sexistes.<br><br>Valeur de l'initiative et l'imagination face à la création d'emploi. |

35

Table 2: Design of a Unit of work.

| Gagner sa vie | | | | |
|---|---|---|---|---|
| Objectives | Sociocultural Contents | Linguistic Contents | Learning Autonomy Contents | Documents |
| 1- To make the students sensitive towards a subject that can be connected with their personal future<br>2- To revise and expand previously acquired knowledge on expository and conversational texts<br>3- To acquire sociocultural knowledge related with work and the way work is organized<br>4- To write letters applying for a job<br>5- To learn how to act in a job interview where knowledge of French is demanded | - Information of the type 'civilization':<br>·youth and first job<br>·agricultural and industrial jobs<br>·type of studies and job<br>·ways of organizing jobs<br>-Representations and connotations<br>·young men and young women facing work<br>·sexual stereotypes in the representations about work and professions | - Superstructure and functions of the expository texts<br>·description of a process<br>- Superstructure of the description<br>·new and given information in the descriptions<br>·characterization of places, people and actions<br>·adjectives<br>·relatives<br>- Letters as a specific way of interaction | - Formulation of personal and group objectives in relation with the sociocultural contents<br>- Observation and analysis of texts in order to infer syntactic rules and to find regularities and patterns<br>- Conceptualization of the way the linguistic elements work in texts<br>- Definition of criteria to evaluate texts<br>- Self assessment and peer assessment from the criteria created<br>- Analysis of the learning strategies used | -Videotapes<br>·young people who want to be singers<br>·advertisements<br>-Newspaper Article<br>·type of studies and their work possibilities<br>-Literary texts<br>·R. Merle<br>·C. Etcherelli<br>-Film<br>·fragment of a F. Truffaut film<br>-Picture<br>·Van Gogh painting<br>-Handouts<br>·surveys<br>·matrices for Role play<br>·application letters |

# References

Benadava, S. (1982) "De la civilisation à l'éthnocommunication". *Le Français dans le monde* n° 170. Paris: Hachette Larousse.

Byram, M. (1990) "Socio-cultural objectives for modern language learning at advance levels" in Report on Workshop 1A.

Byram, M. (1992) *Culture et éducation en langue étrangère.* Paris: Hatier - Didier. Coll. LAL.

Clark, J. L. (1987) *Curriculum renewal in school foreign languages learning.* Oxford: OUP.

Diari Oficial de la Generalitat Valenciana. N° 1759 Curriculum de la Educación Secundaria Obligatoria. Valencia 6- 4- 1992.

Leblanc, C., Courtel, C., Trescases, P. (1990) *Le syllabus culture. Etude Nationale sur les programmes de français de base.* Ottawa: ACPL + M.

Lussier, D. (1992) *Evaluer les apprentissages dans une approche communicative.* Paris: Hachette coll. F.

Report on Workshop 1A *'Curriculum development for modern languages in upper secondary, general, technical and vocational education 15/16 - 18/19'.* Rolduc, Kerkrade (Netherlands), October 1990. Doc. CC-LANG (91) Workshop 1A. Compiled and edited by G. Stoks.

Valdes, J.M. (Red.) (1986) *Culture bound: bridging the gap in language teaching.* Cambridge: CUP.

Zarate, G. (1983) "Du dialogue des cultures à la démarche interculturelle". in *Le Français dans le monde* n° 170. Paris: Hachette Larousse.

Zarate, G. (1990) "L'immersion en contexte étranger: dispositifs de formation et d'évaluation". *Etudes de Linguistique Appliquée* n° 80. Paris: Didier.

# SATELLITE TV:
# A FLEXIBLE LEARNING ENVIRONMENT TO PROMOTE
# CULTURAL AWARENESS

*Daniela SORANI and Anna Rita TAMPONI, Italy*

## The context

In the Italian school system curricula are fairly flexible and their definition is left to the individual Consiglio di Classe (i.e. the teachers of a single class). Nevertheless, the Ministry of Education, at a national level, indicates general guidelines as to the aims and objectives that have to be reached by students at the various levels of schooling and which are of valuable help to teachers in planning their individual syllabi. In all the programmes for foreign language teaching issued by the Ministry there are indications regarding the teaching of cultural aspects connected with the foreign languages to be learned by students, although their formulation is rather vague and no indication is given as to what should be included and how this aspect of the syllabus should be handled from the didactic point of view. For example, here are the references to the teaching of cultural aspects in the declared objectives of foreign language teaching at lower-secondary school level:

"Lo studio della lingua straniera contribuirà ad allargare gli orizzonti culturali, sociali e umani dell'allievo per il fatto stesso che ogni lingua rispecchia i diversi modi di vivere delle comunità che la parlano ed esprime in modo diverso i dati dell'esperienza umana. Esso riveste quindi una grande importanza nell'educazione alla comprensione ed al rispetto degli altri e dei valori che essi posseggono... L'impegno degli allievi allo studio della lingua straniera dovrà essere stimolato dall'interesse a confrontare la propria realtà socio-culturale con quella degli altri Paesi della società contemporanea. Per sviluppare tale motivazione e perché il nesso lingua-cultura sia reso evidente, è essenziale che si parta dalla vita di oggi e soprattutto dalla lingua di oggi. Lo studio della civiltà straniera non deve essere quindi inteso come apprendimento di mere nozioni storiche o geografiche, ma come una presa di coscienza dei valori socio-culturali e dei costumi delle altre comunità tramite la lingua stessa ed attraverso documenti autentici di attualità e di vita quotidiana."[1]

---

[1]    Ministero della Pubblica Istruzione, Programmi della Scuola Media. "The study of a foreign language will contribute to widen the cultural, social and human horizons of the learners as each language is the mirror of the different ways of living of its speakers and as it expresses differently the data of human experience. It is therefore fundamental in educating students to understand and to respect others and their values.....The students' motivation in the learning of a foreign language will be enhanced by the interest of comparing their own sociocultural reality with that of other countries. To foster this motivation and to make the link between language

As far as the upper-secondary school is concerned, among the various aims indicated for the study of foreign languages in the project of reform of secondary-school curricula, we find:

"... comprensione interculturale non limitata alle manifestazioni più usuali della vita quotidiana, ma estesa a espressioni più complesse della civiltà e agli aspetti più significativi della cultura straniera."[1]

It is clear that, whether in a more specific way as is the case with the lower-secondary or in a more generic way for the upper-secondary, the aims and objectives of foreign language teaching include elements of foreign culture. But the freedom of choice in the teaching process attributed to teachers in the Italian Constitution and the rather vague indications offered by the Ministry imply that teachers are free to approach the teaching of cultural elements in any way they want; while this could represent a positive situation, the result is that, for the most part, they limit themselves to the traditional teaching of aspects of civilization and of literature. This trend is also confirmed by the choice of civilization textbooks of a rather traditional nature and by the topics of civilization which are generally included in coursebooks.

A survey taken among 40 colleagues in in-service training courses has given the following results:

- geography                        38
- institutions and government      40
- social problems                  18
- leisure                          34
- school system                    40
- sports                           30
- history                          22

As teachers and teacher-trainers we agreed with Bateson's idea that:

a cross-cultural learning experience takes place when the individual encounters a different culture and as a result:

---

and culture evident, it is fundamental to start from today's life and, above all, from today's language. The study of foreign civilization must not be understood as the learning of mere historical or geographical notions, but as an awareness of the sociocultural values and of the customs of other communities by means of the language and through the use of authentic documents of current events and daily life."

[1]   Ministero della Pubblica Istruzione, I Programmi Brocca. " ... an intercultural understanding not limited to the more usual manifestations of everyday life, but extended to the more complex expressions of civilization and to the more significative aspects of the foreign culture."

a) examines the degree to which he is influenced by his own culture;

b) understands the culturally derived values, attitudes and outlooks of other people.[1]

We were therefore looking for new ways of raising awareness in both students and teachers of the importance of an understanding and an acceptance of "otherness" as well as a clearer definition of "self" and we came to the conclusion that satellite TV was the answer to all our problems. We therefore decided to initiate action in our school and in in-service teacher-training courses in order to exploit the endless resources offered by satellite TV in the area of culture awareness.

Our participation in Council of Europe Workshop 13 on "Language and culture awareness in language learning/teaching (L2 and L1) for the development of learner autonomy (age 11-18)" allowed us to first plan and then implement an R&D project sponsored by our administration.

## The conceptual framework

Our two-year activities have been based on the recognition that our students possess much more information than we did when we were their age, as a result of exposure to the TV medium, as well as extra-curricular experiences contributing to their general knowledge of the world. Nevertheless, their attitude towards the information they receive is very often unselective and passive. In fact, they cannot question the TV set for clarification and they cannot even show their doubts or observations to anyone because they are often left alone, real victims of the subliminal influence of the TV message itself. In fact, the latter even has the power to modify their habits, their ways of thinking and their *Weltanschaung*.

A positive aspect of mass communications is that the whole world has become a "global village", in which the trans-cultural values unify every aspect of life. But, at the same time, due to the different languages spoken around the world, each country has its own expression and values. We as teachers are witnesses of a strange phenomenon affecting our society: every piece of information broadcast through the TV medium soon becomes a "global" heritage, a sort of "humus" on which personal histories grow. Live messages are as quick as meteorites which come and disappear almost at the same time, but leave an "imprinting" which should be correctly elaborated in order not to destroy and deviate personalities. They are a live representation of our civilization and are "momentum" and history at the same time. TV is therefore a "structuring" system which cannot be ignored at school level.

Constructivism has provided the philosophical background for our activities. In fact, constructivism holds that the world around us cannot exist independently of us since there are many ways of structuring the world, and there are many meanings or perspectives for any event or concept. The role of educators is that of providing the

---

[1]    Bateson J. in Zarate, G. (1992) *Représentations de l'étranger et didactique des langues.*

students with the means not only of experiencing knowledge, but above all of *building* their own vision of reality and of creating representations.

Satellite TV may therefore be seen as an environment students can exploit to build their own vision of reality since we believe that it is extremely important to situate learning in a context which can facilitate the process of learning. Experience is consolidated so that "concepts" are embedded in practice avoiding compartmentalisation of knowledge; in this way hypotheses are generated in the students' mind about models of interpretation of reality since satellite TV represents a flexible tool at their disposal. The model could be represented as follows:

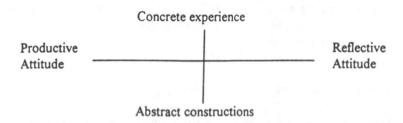

We have used an ethnographic approach to identify characteristics and categories through long term observations (i.e. audio and video tapes and field notes), interviews, written documents and microanalysis of interactions. Special emphasis has been devoted to "the co-construction of knowledge" and to the creation of a low-anxiety atmosphere. Thus, the use of satellite TV programs has acted has an equaliser reducing the gap between the most-talented and less-talented students since both groups co-operated to achieve the tasks and to build their own representations, according to their learning styles and to their individual intelligences.

## The project

The project we carried out was part of a wider project on *How to develop learner autonomy through the use of media* which included both the use of telematics and satellite TV. In our school and in our in-service training courses we focused our attention on the possibilities offered by satellite TV. In order to attain our aim we tried to give an experiential dimension to our project, both as regards the awareness of the potentialities of the TV medium and the differences in the perception of other cultures. Of course, while progressing with our activities, we tried to shift from an affective perspective to a cognitive one. Our objectives were the following:

- to consider the cultural dimension of learning about/acquiring a foreign culture;
- to become aware of cultural diversities;
- to reflect upon one's own culture through a comparison with other cultures;
- to assess possible modifications of one's representations about the foreign culture.

Here are the activities we planned:

- pedagogical experiences with two initial pilot classes of upper secondary school in our institution;
- pedagogical experiences with 35 classes (25 upper secondary, 10 lower secondary) in the district;
- a 20-hour in-service course for teachers of English, French, German and Spanish on the use of satellite TV for the development of language and culture awareness in our institution;
- a 50-hour in-service course for teachers of English on the use of satellite TV for the development of culture awareness in the district.

## Preparatory phases

*a.    Negotiation*

The first two pilot classes showed  great enthusiasm in discussing the possibility of using TV at school on a regular basis, in order to get in touch with  other  cultures. Both classes had already used TV for  language development  for one year.  We used a snow-ball activity to allow the students to express their preference about the foreign country to be investigated.  The majority of the students chose the U.S., although some interest was also expressed about  life in Great Britain.

The negotiation with the teacher-trainees concerned the advantages and disadvantages of using TV as a teaching tool, the approach to use in the classroom and the trainees' expectations.  The majority agreed that recording programmes would be more effective than watching live ones while dealing with culture.  They were also given a questionnaire to elicit their interest in using the TV medium to raise students' cultural awareness and to create active viewers.  The answer was positive in the majority of cases (38/40).  Then the teachers were asked to co-operate in creating a questionnaire for their students about their viewing habits.

*b.    The medium*

The result was that all of the students declared that watching TV is part of their daily life (teenagers watch TV at least 3 hours a day, younger students watch it for longer periods) and often, besides having a TV set at home, they have one in their own bedroom. They mainly choose programmes by either zapping or following their friends' hints and they often do something  else while watching and generally watch alone, although they enjoy  discussing the programmes they liked with friends. They do not often record their programmes and they prefer music videos, commercials, films, serials and soap-operas, which give them information about life and behaviour in other countries. They believe that films and serials contribute to modify their habits, although they are aware that information on TV is not always true. All of the students think that watching TV at school could be challenging to help them interpret the information they receive. The result of the questionnaire confirmed our assumption that educators should be concerned with the impact that TV messages have on teenagers in the construction of their vision of the world  (see Appendix 1).

*c.* *The concept of culture*

Students were invited to form groups and to complete a spidergram centred on the concept of culture using a brainstorming technique. Here is a sample of some of the ideas that prevailed:

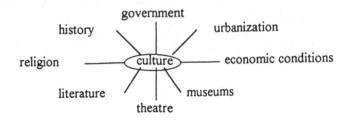

Then students were provided with several definitions of culture and asked to compare them with their ideas and to choose the definition they found most corresponded to their initial assumptions. Here is an example of the definitions we offered:

> culture n.1.a. The totality of socially transmitted behaviour patterns, arts, beliefs, institutions, and all other products of human work and thought. b. These patterns, traits, and products considered as the expression of a particular period, class, community, or population. c. These patterns, traits, and products considered with respect to a particular category, such as a field, subject, or mode of expression. 2. Intellectual and artistic activity, and the works produced by it. 3.a. Development of the intellect through training or education. b. Enlightenment resulting from such training or education. 4. A high degree of taste and refinement formed by aesthetic and intellectual training. 5. Special training and development.[1]

Many of the students realised that originally they had had a rather limited vision of what to include in the concept of culture and were happy to include other areas they had previously ignored.

The same procedure was followed with the teachers involved in in-service courses, but the teachers were also asked to compare their conclusions regarding the concept of culture with the list of cultural topics they had compiled in the original survey. In many cases there was quite a bit of discrepancy between the two.

*d.* *Ethnocentricity level*

In this phase we attempted to diagnose the students' level of ethnocentricity and to make their initial representations of the foreign culture explicit. We interviewed the

---

[1]    American Heritage Dictionary

students and recorded their interviews on individual cassettes that the students themselves kept for further reference. We later had some misgivings about the use of an interview because we felt that the interviewer (the teacher) could act as a filter and that students would either not feel free to express their opinions frankly or else would try to give answers to please the teachers. We therefore tried, the following year with different classes, to replace the interview with a questionnaire which would definitely have a higher degree of objectivity. But we later felt that, in any case, the interview was capable of supplying a greater amount of information due to its less rigid structure and, therefore, that what was gained was more than what was lost. We selected some areas to analyses in the interviews and picked all the adjectives or locutions expressing the students' personal attitude towards the foreign culture. Here is a table that gives an idea of what the initial 40 students (16-years old) said about their perception of various aspects of life in Britain and the U.S.:

| | Britain | U.S.A |
|---|---|---|
| people | reserved, cold, distant | childish, easy-going, noisy, fat |
| climate | cold, rainy, foggy | sunny |
| food | lousy, tasteless, fat | fastfood, hamburgers, fries |
| work | like Italy | hard workers, change jobs |
| religion | Anglicans, Catholics | Catholics, many sects |
| clothes | formal, punk | casual, poorly dressed |
| money | like Italians | rich |
| education | like Italians | uncultivated, very specialised |

The learning module

The didactic module we devised implied different phases. The sample didactic unit we describe below refers to the topic of 'poverty'. Other topics selected concerned sororities and fraternities, students carrying weapons at school, eating habits and in particular anorexia and bulimia, casual vs. formal wear, religious attitudes, family relationships.

PHASE 1:  Exploration of the students' experiential-affective dimension related to a selected aspect of culture, i.e. poverty. (Brainstorming ).
Teachers organise a vocabulary network around a key-word with cultural implications to elicit students' previous experience and students' associated ideas (see Appendix 2).
Role of teacher: observer, monitor.

PHASE 2:  Exploration of the students' cognitive dimension about a selected aspect of culture, i.e. overview of class knowledge and perceptions about poverty.

45

Teachers ask specific questions, students answer (pair or group work) (see Appendix 3).
Role of teacher: observer, monitor

PHASE 3: After the first two phases, the students have been shown a recorded reportage (about 5 minutes in length) on new forms of poverty, in particular regarding white poverty in rural areas of the U.S.
Viewing to understand. (factual and inferential questions). Teachers prepare a factual questionnaire, students answer (see Appendix 4).
Role of teacher: mediator between the TV message and the students.

PHASE 4: Relating initial representations to information acquired by means of the TV medium. (Questionnaire on acquired knowledge, experiential and affective dimension leading to cultural awareness). Teachers deliver questionnaire, students answer (see Appendix 5).
Role of teacher: observer, monitor, resource person.

PHASE 5: Definition of "self". With the support of other subject-matter teachers, students have carried out research work on the levels of poverty in Italy and on various forms of governmental and non-governmental aid projects. This work has also been done also through a comparison with other media (newspapers, magazines, books)
Role of teacher: observer, monitor, resource person

PHASE 6: Changing attitudes towards the use of the medium.
Inter-learner interactions during the activities helped them build their interpretative strategies in decision-making moments and in team-work. Students have become more and more accustomed to decoding the multi-semantic levels of the TV message and have realised the importance of an in-depth analysis, including elements such as the type of camera shots, the interviewer's attitude and voice, colours and sounds, and others.

## Evaluation

It is clear that evaluating students's evolution in attitudes and perceptions is an extremely complex task. Therefore, we found it more advisable to evaluate students at the end of each module for what concerned factual knowledge (see Appendix 5) and analytical and critical approach by means of a unifying practical assignment implying a personal elaboration (reports, presentation of portfolios,...).

At the end of a whole year during which this type of work was carried out, the students were asked to listen to the ethnocentricity interview they had recorded at the beginning of the year and to confirm, modify or even change their attitudes radically. Many of the students admitted that their initial representations on the foreign culture (U.S.) had been rather superficial and probably dictated by stereotypes and prejudices. The majority of them stated that their perception of the "other" had become more complex and articulate and that this work had also helped them clarify what being Italian meant to them.

46

## Conclusions

The creation of individuals who are able to choose, compare and respect "others" should be of primary importance in the promotion of a "democratic" and non-violent attitude towards life and people.

With satellite TV teachers have access to authentic and up-to-date material to be used in the classroom through both an affective and a cognitive dimension; it can activate the learning process and can help create an appealing and flexible learning environment.

From what has been discussed, it is clear that the emphasis is on students' own experience as the starting point for their work and as a basis for comparison with their studies of other cultures. The proposed model proposed considers the learner as a researcher who carries out fieldwork on the foreign culture through the TV medium. In fact, our aim as teachers should be to develop a particular mode of thinking and of reacting to the medium by methods of cultural analysis rather than ready-made reports on stereotyped aspects of mainstream culture, thus suggesting a close link between "experience" and "awareness". Therefore, the difference in attitudes is given an experiential and affective dimension in the final stage of the module, thus shifting from an affective dimension in the first stage, to a cognitive one in the following stages, back to an affective one in the final stage. Moreover, our idea is to promote a non-stereotyped and non-ethnocentric view of the different variables which build up cultures all over the world so that learners become aware of sharing common experiences with other people.

Students can thus develop techniques and strategies they can apply independently to other aspects of English or American life and society, or of other countries and cultures.

# References

Altheide, D. (1976) *Creating Reality. How TV News Distort Event.* London: Sage.

Bettetini, G. (ed.) (1994) *Teoria della Comunicazione*, Franco Angeli.

Byram, M. & Esarte-Sarries, V. (1991) *Investigating Cultural Studies in Foreign Language Teaching*, Clevedon: Multilingual Matters.

Byram, M., Esarte-Sarries, V. & Taylor, S. (1991) *Cultural Studies and Language Learning: a Research Report*, Clevedon: Multilingual Matters.

Byram, M., Morgan, C. et al. (1994) *Teaching and Learning Language and Culture*, Clevedon: Multilingual Matters.

Duffy, J. (1992) *Constructivism and the Technology of Instruction: a Conversation.* New York: Lawrence Erlbaum Associates.

Girotti, M.R., Stefani, P., Rice, R. & Roberts, D. (1991) *Understanding Cultures*, Loescher.

Lancien, T. (ed.) (1994) *Médias: Faits et Effets,* Paris: EDICEF.

Ministére de l'Education Nationale (1990) *Langues et Télévisions par Satellite*, Atelier de Dijon.

Ministero della Pubblica Istruzione (1979) *Programmi della scuola media.*

Ministero della Pubblica Istruzione (1988) *Programmi Brocca.*

Report on Workshop 13A/Rapport de l'Atelier 13A '*Language and culture awareness in language teaching (L2 and L1) for the development of learner autonomy (age 11-18)/Sensibilisation à la langue et à la culture dans l'apprentissage/enseignement des langues (L1 et L2) et développement de l'autonomie de l'apprenant (11-18 years).*' Santa Margerherita Ligure (Genova/Gênes), Italy/Italie, December/décembre 1993. Doc. CC-LANG (95) Workshop 13A/Atelier 13A. Compiled and edited by/coordonné par F. Palamidesi Cesaretti/N. Galli De'Paratesi.

Valdes, J.M. (ed.) (1986) *Culture Bound*, Cambridge: Cambridge University Press.

Zarate, G. 1992, *Représentations de l'étranger et didactique des langues,* Paris: Didier.

# APPENDIX 1

<u>QUESTIONNAIRE</u>

1.  Are you interested in TV?
    <> yes
    <> no
    If not, why?

2.  How many TV sets have you got at home?

3.  Have you got your own TV set?

4.  How do you choose your TV programmes?
    <> TV magazines          <> zapping
    <> friends' hints        <> other

5.  You choose a programme mainly because:
    <> you want to relax and be entertained
    <> you want to be informed
    <> you learn how to behave
    <> you want to discuss the programme with friends
    <> you like the language used
    <> a teacher told you
    <> other

6.  Do you watch TV alone?
    <> yes
    <> no

    If not, with:
    - members of family
    - friends
    - other

7.  How often do you watch TV?

8.  What time of the day do you watch TV?

9.  How long do you watch TV for?

10. What do you do while watching TV?
    <> eat              <> fall asleep      <> pay attention
    <> do homework      <> other

11. Do you record your favourite programmes?
    <> yes
    <> no
    Give reasons for your answer.

12. Would you like to watch TV at school?
    <> yes
    <> no
    Give reasons for your answer.

13. What are your favourite programmes?
    <> cartoons          <> documentaries          <> sports
    <> soap operas       <> scientific programmes  <> news
    <> commercials       <> shows                  <> serials
    <> video music       <> movies                 <> other
    <> talk shows        <> weather forecast

14. The programmes you watch give you more information about:
    <> science           <> life                   <> economy & finance
    <> social problems   <> other countries        <> other
    <> behaviour         <> domestic policy
    <> ethnic groups     <> foreign policy

15. What programmes do you think contribute most to your personal development?

16. What  programmes do you think contribute to modify your personal behaviour?

17. Do you think that information on TV is:
    <> always true    <> often true    <> sometimes true    <> never true

# APPENDIX 2

## PHASE 1 -BRAINSTORMING

KEY-WORD : **Poverty**

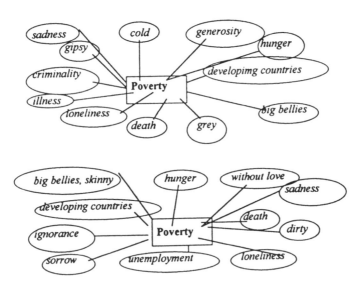

# APPENDIX 3

## PHASE 2 - QUESTIONS

1) What do you consider to be poor countries?
   *Africa, China, Romania, Yugoslavia, Albania, parts of South America, India*

2) Do you think of Americans as being poor?
   *North Americans are rich, South Americans are poor*

3) What percentage of US citizens do you think are below poverty level?
   *10%*

4) What percentage of Italians do you think are below poverty level?
   *30%*

5) Do you associate any particular ethnic group with poverty?
   *Black people, Gypsies, Eskimos.*

6) What is done in Italy for the poor?
   *Volunteer associations, Charitas, Red Cross.*

# APPENDIX 4

<u>PHASE 3 - QUESTIONNAIRE</u>

1) How old are the people presented in the reportage?

2) What do they eat?

3) How much do they earn?

4) Why do they receive this money?

5) Where do they live?

6) How do they survive?

7) How does the US Government deal with the problem of poverty?

8) What is the National Food Bank?

9) Has the poverty rate increased or decreased since 1989?

10) Does poverty have the same connotation in developed and developing countries?

# APPENDIX 5

## PHASE 4 - QUESTIONNAIRE

1) How are the news presented?
   - by speaker
   - by reportage
   - by graphs
   - by interviews with:
     • experts
     • common people
     • politicians

2) What new information did you acquire from the news?
   - about your country
   - about the foreign country
   - about international affairs
   - about humanitarian acts
   - about........

3) Is the speaker's attitude:
   - neutral
   - partisan

5) What is the reaction of
   - experts
   - common people

6) Are their reactions
   - in agreement with your expectations
   - in contrast with your expectations

7) Do you think your reactions are due to:
   - previous knowledge
   - prejudices
   - stereotypes
   - the type of presentation chosen

8) Has this analysis changed your attitude towards the topic discussed?

9) If you were a journalist, how would you report the same news?

# RAISING CULTURAL AWARENESS
# AMONG FOREIGN LANGUAGE TEACHER TRAINEES

*Säde-Pirkko NISSILÄ, Finland*

## Introduction

Internationalisation and European integration are challenges to foreign language education in schools. Its main challenge is to teach relevant communicative competence. Language teachers are in the key position. They should be conscious of the real essence and deep connection of language and culture both in their own and foreign cultural contexts. They should also understand the symbolic system of the target language sufficiently well to be able to guide their students to know it. The fact that culture is intertwined with language should be consciously remembered throughout language studies.

In foreign language education distinction can be made between intercultural competence, understanding and communication (Kaikkonen, 1993). Intercultural *competence* contains the idea that cultures exert influence on each other. However, the learner should use the target language in the authentic way, not mixing foreign words with his native language phrases, for instance. Further, intercultural *understanding* implies that the interpretation is directed by the interpretational codes of the target language, not of the learner's own language. Intercultural *communication* in language education strives to create the qualifications for real communication with another language and culture.

Schein (1987) divides culture into three levels. On the surface level there are artefacts and creations, technology, art, material culture, language and perceivable behaviour, corresponding to the behaviouristic definition. The second level includes values, attitudes and norms which can be explicitly described to show the reasons for and background of the phenomena of the first level. This corresponds to the functional definition of culture. The deepest, unconscious and invisible cultural level includes fundamental assumptions such as the people's relationship to environment, nature, other people, time, space and even their position in the universe. The mastery of the third level is expected from specialists in the field, in this case language teachers.

Often the learner is aided to recognise the features included in levels one and two, in other words, culture oriented behaviour, and to act on its terms. Thus language and culture, language and behaviour are bound together. The danger in making this kind of connection is false conclusions, if the observer interprets foreign behaviour from his own cultural background. The mental processes behind the phenomena should also be understood, for culture is always connected with the individual's conceptions of the world.

In Finland the study by Myllyniemi et al (1992) indicates that many in-service language teachers have a rather limited or problematic conception of culture, although they appreciate, in theory, the connection of language and culture in school teaching. On the other hand, in-service primary English teachers expressed explicitly their need for training in the area of teaching intercultural communication (Nissilä 1995a).

Robinson asked in his study (1988) how teachers of English (ESL and EFL) defined culture. Most answers explained it either behavioristically or functionally. According to the first concept teachers listed observable features of behaviour: language, gestures, customs, food, as well as products, literature, folklore, art, music and artefacts. They described also observable behaviour, like family-life, free-time activities or buying food, not explaining why they happen.

Functional definitions concerned conceptions, i.e. beliefs, values and institutions. This focus was on the reasons and rules of behaviour. Less frequently did the teachers explain culture by a cognitive or symbolistic definition, such as the world-view, a conception which teachers were not even able to clarify (Robinson, 1988).

According to the cognitive definition, culture is the logic by which people analyses, organise and understand the world. The mental view includes the claim that culture is not a material phenomenon and does not comprise matter, things and behaviour, but their models and shapes which are stored in people's memory. Thus this point of view stresses the information processing. The difficulty lies in the fact that it is not easy to collect research data concerning people's emotional experiences. Culture is, however, connected also with emotions.

The symbolistic definition explains culture as a system of symbols emphasising the outcomes and meanings of information processing. According to the symbolistic view the task of foreign language teaching is to create in a student a system of foreign language symbols and senses including the linguistic expressions and communication strategies of the target language (Byram, 1989).

Learning a foreign language and culture can also be observed as social and individual phenomena. The social viewpoint refers to the set of values, rules and meanings which are shared by the members of a community and which control their behaviour, acts and products. This point of view describes culture as the learned, not inherited, collective programming of the mind. In this sense culture is not individual but collective, although every individual has his own meanings and interpretations (Hofstede 1980).

From an individual point of view, culture is a process of learning symbols and meanings, which process is influenced by individual prior knowledge: previous conceptions, information and experiences. The meanings given to symbols inform the interpretations. The interpretation directs the next experience, which provides new contents to the meaning. This process is deeply individual. In this study the individual, as well as the social processes will be approached through introspective, retrospective and reflective documents of teacher trainees whose systematic increase of cultural awareness was examined during the academic year of 1994-1995. This report will tell how the theme of language and culture was presented and worked on.


## Design of the Study

This study is a part of a more comprehensive research project the aim of which is to explore the means of promoting cultural and intercultural aspects in foreign language teaching. The first task is to make in-service and pre-service language teachers conscious of the concepts connected with culture and aware of the activities which promote intercultural learning. Because professional development is often slow and unnoticed, the changes are not easily documented. In this report they are approached mainly through the documented reflection of teacher trainees for secondary schools.

*Reflective self-assessment in developing cultural awareness*

Within the framework of experiential learning (Kolb 1984) it is possible to understand changes in teachers and teacher trainees. Learning is seen as a cyclic process of integrating concrete experience, reflective observation, abstract conceptualisation and active experimentation into balanced and holistic understanding. Kohonen (1992, 42) writes: "Practice, reflection, theory and action belong essentially to professional development. Learning is seen as a continually sharpening and deepening change of knowledge, as the re-learning of a previously learnt matter on a deeper level of understanding and consciousness." The changes do not take place automatically; they require courage to encounter problems, solve them and evaluate personal action. The changes imply co-operation with colleagues.

Experiential learning promotes the development of learner autonomy and metacognitive skills. The autonomous learner is able to make independent decisions, plans, implementations and evaluations. Metacognitive skills aid the learner to master and direct his knowing and skills in a concentrated way (e.g. Oxford, 1990).

Research projects which have investigated the development of pre-service and in-service teachers show that teachers undergo changes both during their teacher training period and after it (e.g. Niemi et al., 1995). Reflective comments and notions upon the experiences, interaction and learning outcomes can be documented for instance by writing a diary. Finding words to express the emotions raised by the experience clarifies the processes of thinking, learning and evaluation. Together with the substance, the material which is being worked on, the reflective practice becomes more focused (Nissilä, 1995b).

The following sections show how foreign language teacher trainees' reflective practices during the training programme changed their conceptions of culture, of cultural education and of their own cultural awareness.

*The problems, subjects and method of the study*

The purpose of this empirical study was to find answers to the following question:

How can a foreign language teacher trainee for secondary schools acquire such awareness and competence in intercultural communication that he will later be capable of joining the intercultural aspect to his own teaching at school?

To explore the phenomenon, a sequence of successive actions were designed. The findings concerning the trainees' thinking, attitudes and awareness come mainly from the reflection documents.

The subjects of the study consisted of 34 foreign language (English, German, Swedish) students who participated in the subject teacher's pedagogical studies, consisting of educational science, didactics and teaching practice, in the academic year of 1994-1995. This was their fifth year of studies. In the previous years they had studied in the philological faculty. The trainees were not told beforehand that they formed a project group. In this way the findings were expected to be as natural as possible. It often happens that when students know where the focus of observations lie, they concentrate on those aspects in a way which would not happen otherwise.

The research method was qualitative. The documentation of thinking and attitudes of the trainees was analysed with the help of content analysis. In the inductive analysis the analysis unit was an utterance (comprising one thought, i.e. either one word, group of words or sentence). The units were re-arranged in thematic categories. The thematic analysis had the same aim: to arrange the utterances which express the same idea or theme under the common title. The categories of both analyses fell mainly together. Statistical measures were not used, because the material and method are more suitable to descriptive reporting.

*Aims*

The main problem of this study, how to raise the cultural awareness of the foreign language teacher trainees for secondary schools, was divided into sub-questions leading to the definition of the goals. Thus the purpose of this study was:

1. to make a trainee conscious of the concept of culture and other concepts connected with it (cultural competence, intercultural understanding, learning and communication, national and foreign images of culture etc.) from the point of view of foreign language teaching;

2. to start an active personal reflection process on the cultural aspects in school teaching;

3. to make a trainee analyses his/her own process of increasing consciousness and deepen it;

4. to plan classroom activities to develop a trainee's cultural knowledge and skills both in theory and practice;

5. to describe how the project was realised throughout the period;

6. to find out how cultural competence developed during the project, and

7. to chart the measures which seemed to deepen the cultural competence of a trainee and his/her readiness to teach intercultural communication.

The research material was collected during a relatively short period, when speaking of developmental processes. On the other hand, all the trainees had some kind of preconceptions, more or less consciously. The interpretations of the research data are connected with the researcher's own conceptions of culture and foreign language learning. They are based on theoretical studies and practical personal experiences as well as on a career as a language teacher and teacher educator.

*Research procedures*

The research procedures were the following:

1. widening the researcher's own competence on this special area:

   - in national workshops arranged by the National Board of Education and Teacher Education Institutes of Finland during the period of 1992-1995;

   - through consulting international researchers and experts on this field;

   - by reading professional literature on the topic.

2. planning the project together with the co-researchers on the national level, as well as planning the separate procedures together with the trainees.

3. carrying out the project.

4. documenting the trainees' conceptions, planning and learning outcomes as well as the observation notes of the researcher.

6. analysing the research data, drawing conclusions and writing a report.

**Figure 1. The description of the project**

| BACKGROUND MEASURES |
| :---: |
| of the researcher: |
| national workshops<br>reading professional literature<br>definition of the concept of intercultural learning collaboratively |

| THE PLAN |
| :---: |
| to increase cultural awareness among the teacher trainees,<br>taking into account their preconceptions |

| THE REALISATION OF THE PLAN | THE DOCUMENTATION |
| :--- | :--- |
| Autumn 1994 | |
| Instruction (lectures, workshops, etc.) and a test. | Test papers on didactics, reflection diaries. |
| Simulation exercises. | Oral and literal products, observations. |
| Writing and presenting an essay on professional literature. | Essays and observations of group discussions. |
| Reflection diary and portfolio. | Diaries, notes, interviews. |
| Spring 1995 | |
| Planning topic-based tasks. | Lesson and action plans, observations of group discussions. |
| Designing and carrying out an empirical study on language teaching. | Research papers. |
| Reflective self-assessment of one's own research process. | Questionnaires. |
| A self-assessment of cultural awareness and teaching. | Questionnaires. |
| Reflection diary and portfolio. | Diaries, notes, interviews. |

| INVESTIGATION AND REPORT |
| :---: |
| qualitative content analysis<br>thematic arrangement of the data<br>report |

# Analysing Trainee Teachers' Cultural Knowledge and Skills

The investigation of the reflection material shows that the connection of language and culture was not self-evident to the students when coming to teacher education. Though their previous studies had emphasised linguistic skills, they were now positive towards the goal of including cultural aspects in language lessons. In fact, they are also obliged to do this by the national curriculum which includes the ideas of cultural understanding, intercultural communication and the meeting of cultures (National Board of Education, 1994. Framework Curriculum for the Comprehensive School).

When comparing the trainees' thinking with the model by Schein, during and after the project, their awareness seems to cover the behaviouristic and functional levels. The third and highest level has been attained by only a few trainees, as became clear from the questionnaires and the observer's notes in group discussions. The highest level of cultural understanding and competence is the goal of language teacher education.

*Concept of culture*

The concept of culture as well as other concepts linked with it became more definite to everyone, as mentioned above. The aspects typical of levels one and two appeared in all documents. In the questionnaires on cultural awareness the trainees wrote almost unanimously that the most important areas of intercultural communication are language, customs/habits/manners and values/norms, because:

> 'You have to know the language sufficiently to be able to get a contact to a person representing another culture. If you know how to act in different situations, it makes communication easier. Values are always essential in every language and culture.'

This kind of pragmatic view of successful communication dominated the answers. Only a few of the trainees came to think of the concept more profoundly. A trainee who has lived in the target country had a wider perspective, but not yet full consciousness of the deeper meaning of culture:

> 'I think language, customs and values are the most important areas of culture, because they are most closely linked with communication. The other areas (social structures, geography, history, literature and arts, science and technology, politics and economy) depend more on the interests of the speaker. Knowing or not-knowing them does not necessarily promote communication or, on the other hand, cause communication breaks.'

In other contexts all the trainees emphasised that teaching culture is an integral part of language teaching.

*Cultural aspects in a language classroom*

The process of becoming aware of cultural aspects in school teaching was amply documented, which shows that nobody remained untouched. They seemed to be most deeply affected by the lectures and workshops on teaching immigrant students, as the following extracts tell:

> 'Nowadays I consider the teaching of culture more important than ever, for culture is an important part of language and contacts. Also the teaching of immigrants is very important, so that it would be easier for them to get familiar with the new culture.'

> 'I am now aware of the fact that my cultural knowledge is rather scanty. I have not got much experience of the immigrants either, but I have seen in practice how racist Finns can be.'

To discuss some of the cultural aspects of language teaching more thoroughly the reflection material will be dealt with in three sections: language knowledge, sociocultural competence and strategic competence.

*Language knowledge and culture*

Language knowledge is often defined as an ability to use language appropriately in language-based situations (e.g. Bachman 1990). The fields that will be discussed here are grammatical and discourse competences. Grammatical competence consists of morphology, syntax, lexis, semantics, phonology, and intonation (Canale & Swain 1980). They are all necessary for communication, but trainees feel that lexical mistakes tend to cause more communication breaks than other grammatical errors. In addition, the choice of words is a culture-based feature:

> 'Learning the words is important, because their role in communication is significant. To be able to take part in a discussion a foreign language learner must first be able to recognise the key words and then produce himself the words he needs to express his own thoughts. ... Communication will break totally, if people don't use the right words in a discussion. ... Outside the classroom the negative reactions against wrong words are much stronger than against grammatical mistakes.'

Although lexical competence is important in communication, the teaching of structures has traditionally been emphasised in Finland. A trainee came to the following conclusion:

> 'The starting point of most of the texts is to teach grammar. Therefore the cultural contribution is limited. The texts contain everyday dialogues between the characters, and the events could take place almost anywhere.'

On the other hand the proper amount of grammar leads to accuracy of expression. Accuracy is one end of the continuum with fluency at the other end. In trainees' opinion, the emphasis on grammar sometimes leads to the phenomenon that school students' compositions, as well as their oral presentations, can be full of grammatically correct, but socioculturally incorrect expressions. A trainee cautiously recommends translation as a conscious medium to teach grammar and communicational skills:

'Practising translation might seem different, if it could be seen from the cultural point of view, as a medium of learning culture.'

General discourse functions are first learnt in the mother tongue, which possibly makes learning a new language easier. On the other hand, the matter is not so easy: different languages have their own culture-bound features which are derived from general norms. For instance, Finnish reticence, i.e. listening silently to what is told, is felt to be polite among Finns, but impolite and uninterested from an Anglo-American perspective. Even worse is the tendency to avoid communication for fear of making mistakes:

'The very first task for us teachers is to encourage Finns to open their mouths without fear of losing face, as it is always more polite to say something than remain quiet. If we are not born polite, we could at least learn to be so.'

Although the rules of oral communication are culture-bound, there are generally relevant categories of spoken language which the language teacher should at least be aware of. It would help him/her to observe the scope of his/her own teaching. Communication tasks and situational contexts could also be combined which would make the exercises meaningful in the trainees' view.

*Sociocultural competence*

Sometimes it is difficult to discern communication skills from structural competence or from the functional skills and sociocultural competence, because they are present and intertwined in everyday life. Moreover, functional (communication) skills have usually a sociocultural background. In this report an effort has been made to categorise the notes of the trainees by using the term functional skills or competence when emphasising action through language with or without a non-verbal element. Sociocultural skills or competence, on the other hand, underline the cultural context. Nonverbal communication should in many cases be observed also from the sociocultural point of view.

When thinking of the reasons why Finnish pupils are unwilling to practise culturally correct communication in the target language, a trainee supposes that the lack of suitable models might serve as an explanation: school books teach grammar, and the teacher doesn't always aim at culturally genuine communication:

'It would be interesting to investigate the role of English teachers as to how important they consider communicative competence in their teaching, and whether they actually consciously apply it in practice, for instance speak English in the class or use methods which encourage pupils not only to speak spontaneously but also to appreciate other cultures and their differences.'

The lack of personal experience with the target culture often appears in faulty communication habits. Genuine intercultural communication is manifested, e.g., in appropriate nonverbal behaviour which varies from culture to culture. It must:

'absolutely be emphasised in teaching language and culture, and in business life, to mention only a couple of fields. At least the future language teachers in my seminar group are now aware of the significance of non-verbal communication to people 'on the stage' and of how and why it should be noticed in teaching.'

Although there appear different functional models for language use in school books, the trainees suggest that teachers should be critical about the texts they accept for school use and evaluate the cultural knowledge and images presented in them. Teachers should also acquaint themselves with the cultural issues and stereotypes of other subject school books, and be careful that the areas of cultural knowledge which are ignored in school texts should be dealt with in other contexts.

School students' attitudes towards foreign languages are formed by incorporating many influences and impressions (e.g. Laine 1987). The attitude influences the amount of work a school student is willing to do. In Finland the attitudes towards studying Swedish are quite different for obvious historical reasons. Two future Swedish language teachers write:

'The traditional dislike of the neighbouring country affected the answers (of school students) a lot.'

They continued of school students' conceptions of other nations:

'Calling bad names was the more general, the more distant the nationalities which were spoken of. Pupils also compared other nationalities to their own and defined them 'like us' or 'normal', if they were not felt distant. They gave a lot of stereotypic answers, e.g. European people were often associated with positive stereotypes.'

The same teacher trainees concluded:

'In our future job we are going to pay attention to international education so that the pupils' knowledge of and attitudes towards foreign cultures and diversity would be improved.'

Being well informed is very important for a teacher to be able to recognise social phenomena and attitudes. The level of knowledge of Swedish culture was relatively good among the teacher trainees and school students. The pupils' conceptions of Germans were regrettably stereotypic. Over-idealisation of the target country and culture, on the other hand, is not wise, either, as the following comment on an English text-book reveals:

'There are no people from different cultural backgrounds and races... Furthermore, everything is always presented positively, and all the less attractive realities of life are left unmentioned... There is no unemployment, no poverty, no homelessness, no crimes, no pollution. It can be said that the macro-level (social, political and historical matters) is totally absent. All kinds of bigger and smaller problems are non-existent also on the micro-level... The characters do not fight with each other and they are never upset, angry or sad... The texts tell very little about culture in English-speaking countries... The teacher should cover this lack of cultural content with extra - preferably authentic - material.'

To sum up it seems that the trainees have become more aware of and able to analyses the attitudes of school pupils and the materials presented in textbooks. This awareness developed obviously during the intensive period of reading, asking questions, reflecting and writing their seminar paper.

*Culture-based strategic competence*

Strategies are policies which either promote or slow up learning. They can be practised and learnt. Thus the teacher should know how to teach them to pupils. A trainee who studied foreign language communication strategies wrote:

'To myself this research is surprisingly significant. Through the research material which I collected ... I got such messages which I would not have got otherwise. I learnt to understand better how students study and learn, which I can make use of in my own teaching.'

The trainees also paid attention to the critical reading of the texts, which ability is needed in this time of increasing accessibility of information via mass media and electronic communication. Critical evaluation will also guarantee the choice of culturally and linguistically representative teaching materials.

The trainees emphasise that language is not only words and structures, but it is culture-bound behaviour. To evaluate the culturally essential ways of speaking, reacting and, possibly, non-verbal expressions, relevant tests should be designed.

*Cultural aspects of language teaching*

To conclude, all the trainees point out that learning a culture does not happen through one channel only, but is influenced by many factors. They consider it important that cultural aspects should be integrated as widely as possible in all school subjects, especially languages:

> 'Teaching culture mustn't be a separate part isolated from the body of language lessons ... Stereotypes come from many school subjects and their teachers.'

Secondly, the trainees point out the importance of personal contacts and experiences with the target language and culture both for teachers and all levels of students. For instance, non-verbal communication is nearly impossible to learn without real native contacts:

> 'The teacher's ability to teach non-verbal communication presupposes her stay in the target country. It is only there that she gets the best chances to observe and adopt the non-verbal communication characteristic of that culture.'

Personal contacts with the cultures would also diminish the regrettable stereotypes and the possible conflicts caused by them, although travelling in itself does not guarantee cultural tolerance:

> 'we noticed clearly that the pupils who had foreign acquaintances had the most positive attitudes towards that special country, for ... in tourist trips you do not always make contact with the natives. It is difficult to say how much travelling correlates with tolerance.'

The trainees also noted that pupils in schools often said that their knowledge of other cultures comes as much from TV, the cinema and the press as from travel abroad.

Increasing tolerance and allowing diversity are themes which, according to the trainees, do not belong only to language teachers but to everyone in the school staff. In addition, home-life and all adults are responsible for creating positive attitudes towards other cultures. Tolerance and appreciation start from knowing one' own culture first, which can lead to understanding other ways of thinking, acting and restructuring the world.

*Personal development in cultural awareness*

The students were asked to evaluate their attitudes to language and culture at the end of their teacher training period, and compare them with their thinking at the beginning of the academic year. All students stated that it was not until this year that they had understood the close connection between culture and language. They had previously had an undefined idea, although the majority said they had always been culturally oriented in their lives. A couple of students even explained that they had realised that they were actually more interested in culture than in language, while someone else had noticed that her cultural knowledge had been minimal before this year. She had ended up with this conception "after taking part in the topic-based teaching exercises and after looking for material for it in the libraries for days on end".

All respondents mentioned that becoming culturally aware had changed their values and attitudes. For instance, they had become more sensitive to the importance of cultural understanding not only in teaching communicational skills but also in opposing racism, recognising the problems of immigrants and in their readiness to help them to integrate into Finnish society. They had also noticed how important it is to make pupils in schools understand and learn the same.

Some trainees also reflected in this context on the practical measures which could increase the positive attitudes of pupils towards other cultures and make them more tolerant in their daily lives. From the teacher's point of view, a doubtful respondent asked, if too much is now demanded of teachers. She suggested that the official curriculum should be enough, but forgot that intercultural understanding and communication are included in the official goals.

*From awareness to practical classroom activities*

To change awareness into practical measures in teaching started with the <u>simulation exercises</u> (see Jones 1984, 20). They offered experiential material as well as chances to exercise pragmatic competence in a (restricted) autonomous way. This special unit comprised different role-plays which aimed at creating culturally correct interaction. The trainees both tested ready-made tasks and designed new ones.

Oral and written reflections on these exercises were important, because they helped the trainees to verbalise their feelings and analyses them. Through that process a single experience could be raised to a higher, more general level. The trainees noticed that simulation is an effective way of learning culture-bound communication. On the other hand, they are neither easy nor simple. They need a lot of preparation work from the teacher, and enthusiasm and risk-taking from the students. They prepare the participants for real interaction, because they imply real skills in pragmatic competence.

After planning <u>topic-based tasks</u> (see Brewster 1991) all the trainees were convinced that alternative ways of teaching, like the one in question, can bring cultural knowledge into learning situations much better than traditional lessons. They also noticed that the teacher must be really aware of the cultural features which are to be taught to the school students.

When reflecting on their own practice lessons and the cultural input in them, they wrote:

'There were no such situations (i.e. the teacher as the mediator of the target culture). Or maybe there were chances for that, but I did not recognise them.'

'I invited an American footballer to visit the class and talk about the rules of the game.'

Although the practical measures taken in their lessons were scanty, the <u>ideas</u> and plans for their future teaching were richer. Reflecting how to teach cultural aspects at school yielded ideas concerning a) the teacher and her professional skills, b) teaching material, c) methods and d) extra-curricular activities.

## a) The teacher and her professional skills

The trainees considered it important that teachers have as good language and cultural competences as possible and that they are maintained by visiting and staying in the target country, having foreign contacts, and, in general, taking care of their own communicative skills.

When asked about their own sources of cultural information, the trainees' list was the following:

1. mass media, 2. contacts with the target country, 3. university studies, 4. literature, and 5. communication with native-speakers.

A surprising point is that the contacts with the target country and communication with natives are separate. The reason may be that the latter is not equally profitable, because it can happen anywhere, not only in the target country. In general, the trainees recommend "longer stays and compulsory language placements in the target country during university studies".

Another thing to be pointed out is that the influence of modern electronic networks is not reflected upon. Obviously it has not reached this group of humanities students yet; school students are however already well acquainted with them.

## b) Teaching materials

When preparing material for teaching, authors should pay attention to the cultural aspects and availability of the materials:

'The teacher will surely find it easier to move to a more culture-oriented way of teaching, if he need not be without support.'

School texts are often considered either defective in cultural material or the culture is hidden "between the lines" where the teacher has to dig it up, if he is interested enough:

'Mainly the cultural knowledge of schools is scattered, and its only source is school books.'

If the texts do not offer material for, for example, functional exercises, the teacher should find authentic material from other sources and make it suitable for the pupils' needs. On the other hand, the teachers' tendency to ignore other ready-made material except school book chapters also caused some criticism:

'too often the pictures, textbanks etc. are ignored or overlooked, when in fact they would be ideal sources of culture.'

## c) Methods

Teaching methods should develop towards learner-centredness. That's why the trainees recommended role-plays, simulation exercises and a careful choice of topics as well as information packs, videos and authentic audiotapes. They would also invite visitors to lessons and make links with the target country representatives. They would try to make culture consciously a part of their teaching and connect the cultural element with learning situations, for instance:

- by emphasising the values and habits of culture any time the themes allow it.

- by giving up the traditional routines of the lessons. By re-valuing the different activities and sections of lessons.

- by arranging more communicative exercises in the language lessons, for instance role-plays, and not reading the text book all the time.

While most students gave a detailed list of the cultural things that should be included in language lessons, one trainee stressed that school students should be taught to think for themselves and analyses impressions:

'I think one of the most important aims would be to give as realistic a picture as possible and to 'shake' the attitudes and prejudices of the pupils - to make pupils think.'

## d) Extra-curricular activities

References to extra-curricular learning opportunities were many. For instance official contacts between schools in different countries should be encouraged. All personal contacts with the target language speakers as well as hobbies can promote the skills of intercultural communication.

*Change of cultural competence*

As the outline of the project in Figure 1 explained, the procedures were designed to create opportunities for the trainees allowing them to become familiar with the different aspects of culture. Simultaneously with finding definitions and clarifications of culture, the trainees were supposed to develop their perceptions and thinking. How was it manifested in their cultural picture and pedagogical thinking? This aspect was mainly approached from the angle of diary and essay writing, self-evaluation and open-ended questions. The leading idea of the project was to make each student sensitive to the phenomena of culture, able to observe them and compare them with those of his/her own culture.

The cultural knowledge of the trainees increased best, according to their own evaluation, when they carried out their individual research plans and wrote their seminar paper on a language and culture theme. This empirical study in a theoretical framework was a powerful asset: it included reading professional literature, defining the research problem and the ways of approaching it, collecting, analysing and arranging empirical material and drawing the conclusions. Trainees were also expected to reflect upon the significance of their themes and evaluate their own working methods and results.

Prior to the seminar paper, professional literature was connected with a task of writing an argumentative essay on a specific theme and presenting it to co-trainees. Also writing a reflection diary throughout the academic year supported the learning of culture as well as the teaching practise itself. Getting acquainted with teaching materials, methods, aims and school students' attitudes gave the trainees concrete ideas of how to include the aspect of culture in their teaching.

*Recommendations for language teacher education*

The measures which were taken during this project with the trainees (Figure 1) should be taken every year and developed further. Moreover, new projects should be organised systematically, for instance inter-curricular cultural projects. The research themes should cover various aspects of culture. An important thing is also that every trainee should learn how to reflect on his/her conceptions, attitudes and activities both in writing and orally. The latter method offers him/her a chance to share reflection with colleagues, which is a very enriching experience.

Trainees should develop and deepen their awareness of the target cultures both in the theory and practice of cultural, didactic and linguistic expertise as well as through keeping contacts with the target countries. They should be guided to add the cultural aspect in their teaching of different levels and types of classes. Teaching immigrant children seemed to give them a fresh point of view on intercultural communication.

## Conclusion

A pre-service teacher's professional growth implies making implicit things explicit. The level of explicit cultural awareness among the trainees in this report is promising: they should all know by now the necessity of deepening their cultural knowledge and developing their skills in intercultural communication. From the viewpoint of educational interaction the question is: how to increase the skill of teaching cultural competence? The following features became explicit throughout the project:

1. The first demand is on a teacher's professional competence: the teacher has to understand and master intercultural communication and arrange opportunities for the learners for authentic experiences of the target language and culture.

2. Reflection is a key to the internalisation of knowledge: the trainees' conceptions became more definite and comprehensive through reflection. School pupils should also be given time to reflect and talk about their experiences of foreign cultures. Once the process of becoming sensitive to another culture has started, pupils as well as the trainees will continue making observations and resolutions.

3. In teaching culture it is important not to idealise or undervalue other cultures. A realistic attitude will help the learner to make comparisons, which helps him/her to recognise the typical features of another culture.

4. The strictly traditional models and routines of language lessons in Finland should be abandoned where they still exist. Moving to project work, for instance, would give learners opportunities to work on one theme longer. Learner-centred teaching in all its forms can lead to greater autonomy of a learner, which in its turn can provide more meaningful learning experiences.

5. Nothing can, however, surpass the real meeting of cultures! As long as the concrete opportunities are lacking, the learners can be prepared for it by versatile methods and equipment, not to forget videos, multimedia, authentic texts, audiotapes and visitors. The aim of language teaching should be kept in mind: it is to increase intercultural and communicational competences.

## References

Bachman, L. (1990). *Fundamental Considerations in Language Testing*. Oxford: Oxford University Press.

Brewster, J. (1991). "What is good primary practice?" In Brumfit, C., Moon, J. & Tongue, R. (eds) *Teaching English to Children*. London: HarperCollins Publishers.

Byram, M. (1989). *Cultural Studies in Foreign Language Education*. Clevedon: Multilingual Matters Ltd.

Canale, M. & Swain, M. (1980). "Theoretical bases of communicative approaches to second language teaching and testing". *Applied Linguistics* 1/1. pp. 1-40.

Hofstede, G. (1980). *Culture's Consequences: International Differences in Work-Related Values.* London: Sage.

Jones, K. et al (eds) (1984). *Simulationen im Fremdsprachenunterricht.* Munchen: Hueber.

Kaikkonen, P. (1993). *Kulttuuri ja vieraan kielen oppiminen. Tampereen opettajankoulutuslaitoksen julkasuja A16.* Tampere: Tampereen Yliopiston Jäljennepalvelu.

Kohonen, V. (1992). "Restructuring school learning as learner education: toward a collegial school culture and cooperative learning". In Ojanen, S. (1992). *Nordic Teacher Training Congress: Challenges for Teacher's Profession in the 21st Century.* Joensuu: University of Joensuu, Research Reports of the Faculty of Education 44.

Kolb, D. (1984). *Experiential Learning. Experience as the Source of Learning and Development.* Englewood Cliffs: Prentice Hall.

Laine, E. (1987). *Affective Factors in Foreign Language Learning and Teaching. Jyväskylä Cross-Language Studies 44.* Jyväskylä: University of Jyväskylä.

Myllyniemi, M. & Mäkikalli, K. (1992). *Englannin kielen opettajien valmiudet kulttuuriopetuksen toteuttamiseen peruskoulun ala-asteella. Pro gradu -tutkielma.* Turku: Turun opettajan-koulutuslaitos.

National Board of Education (1994). *Framework Curriculum for the (Finnish) Comprehensive School.* Helsinki: Painatuskeskus.

Niemi, H. & Kohonen, V. (1995). *Towards New Professionalism and Active Learning in Teacher Development: empirical findings on teacher education and induction.* Tampere: Tampereen yliopisto.

Nissilä, S-P. (1995a). "Ala-asteen englanninopettajan näkemys kielen oppimisesta ja opettamisesta". In Huttunen, I. & Kukkonen, L. (1995). *Valtakunnallinen ala-asteen 6. luokan englannin koe.* Helsinki: Opetushallitus.

Nissilä, S-P. (1995b) "Looking Forward by Looking Back: Reflective Skills in ITE". A paper read at the ECER Conference 14-17.9.95 in Bath, England.

Oxford, R. (1990). *Language Learning Strategies.* New York: Newbury House Publishers.

Robinson, G.L.N. (1988). *Crosscultural Understanding.* Cambridge: University Press.

Schein, E. (1987). *Organisaatiokulttuuri ja johtaminen.* Espoo: Weilin & Göös.

# PROJECTS AND OTHER TOOLS:
## SOME STRATEGIC REMARKS ON INTERCULTURAL LEARNER COMPETENCE

*Roland FISCHER, Austria*

## Introduction

At all stages of foreign language teaching and learning insight into and deeper understanding for the cultures of the target languages has been a prominent aim - not always explicitly, it is true, (sometimes knowledge of linguistic phenomena, rules and patterns were in the foreground with applicability and cultural understanding just 'by - products') but still, with mobility growing and business becoming more and more global, international language pedagogues and business people alike have come to call for 'intercultural skills', 'practical cultural knowledge' or 'international competence'. Communication deprived of its cultural dimension - as it has shown - remains defective, incomplete and bookish. Especially if 'communication' is synonymous for 'genuine mutual understanding' and is not restricted to the streamlined ritual of technocratic business agenda in a sometimes sterile, 'culture free' environment of a multinational, the cultural dimension of language learning cannot be cut out.

In an attempt to meet the demands of a quick and successful communication flow a number of publications have appeared on the bookshelves that try to supply users with the necessary concise information: adapting behaviour to rituals and social conventions, it is believed, minimises disturbances of the communication flow without having to bother about genuine understanding. and insight. These 'Introduction-into-the-culture-of-...' and 'How-to-deal-with...' paperbacks, admittedly, do provide some practical value. Their principle of reducing 'cultural understanding' to 'familiarity with etiquette', however, fails in creating a sound basis for adequate, conscientious action.

A closer analysis of textbooks and additional supplementary collections of materials reveals three major methods of teaching intercultural skills:

- teachers *presenting* information directly;
- students *gathering* information from different sources;
- *exposure* to authenticity or near-authenticity.

From a language learning point of view the three methods involve a range of communicative learner, i.e. language activities: more limited and one sided in the first case, it is true, with a concentration on comprehension and note taking, leaving the learners mostly in the passive role of 'consumers' of facts and figures. The information on the target cultures is usually referred to as 'representative' and delivered by teachers or lecturers in 'Landeskunde - classes' or is presented in booklets or brochures. They are often of an official character, published by ministries or publicly funded institutions. At any rate the underlying intention of such a method is to deliver a *survey*, to aim at some kind of *completeness* and, above all, to be *objective*. This kind of sociocultural knowledge can be found in books like *'Österreich - Tatsachen und Zahlen'*, which is edited and regularly updated by the public relations department of the Austrian government and published in six different languages. Most European countries offer similar materials.

The second and the third of the above mentioned approaches involve the learners more actively and in a more diversified range of activities. *Information-gathering* could mean: different groups of learners are engaged working with different materials (texts, statistics, interviews, audio-, video- and print materials, literary and journalistic texts etc.), consulting each other, exchanging and comparing their findings, sometimes coming close to an ideal communicative classroom, in which everybody is willing, able and not just 'told' to make some contributions, language and culture learning as a process involving all students, with teacher-facilitators and teacher-organisers rather than traditional leaders.

Similar principles are applied when it comes to *exposing learners to authenticity*. This way of dealing with and learning from foreign cultures is initiated both in L1 and L2 environments: the former is frequently the case when foreign students attend the same classes or when foreign language assistants are sent all over Europe representing a given language, country and culture 'in person', or when other (native speaker) guests are invited into the foreign language classroom. Exposure also happens, when learners deal with current authentic materials, or when problems of a foreign culture (C2) are 'transferred' through simulations or role plays. (e.g. Austrian environmentalists fighting against the building of a hydro-electric power plant in Lambach, a little town in Upper Austria, as a simulation in a German class in Portugal, with all the background information, press coverage etc. necessary.)

Growing European mobility in general, exchange programmes and study trips, internships and short school excursions to foreign countries (with activities of 'erlebte Landeskunde') expose an ever growing number of learners directly and 'authentically' to C2, to foreign life and 'real' facts.

Different as they may be, the above mentioned approaches have one thing in common: they are applied in order to gain, pool, exchange and eventually use information, they *activate language skills*, and in the best of cases they integrate these activities into an (inter)active foreign language classroom

# Intercultural approaches in language teaching

The question remains, however, whether the learners have thus just learned to obtain a certain amount of information or get the 'cultural message' across. In applying for example communicative comprehension skills the learners might be able very successfully to extract or identify 'information' from given sources. This communicative act, however - i.e. Landeskunde based on information alone - is liable to errors and misconceptions for several reasons:

- 'complete' information, which would be required, remains an illusion;
- there are no or hardly any criteria for the validity or 'representativeness' of data;
- all the information learners encounter is pre-selected (and thus manipulated) by teachers or textbook authors;
- the total amount of information is influenced by the learner's L2 proficiency levels, his/her experience, by (accidental) availability and access to sources and other chance factors.

To grasp its full meaning, information has to be seen within the framework of *its own*, not the learner's cultural background and it depends on the learners ability to *place phenomena* within the system of co-ordinates of the *target* culture and *its* set of rules and values. Understanding otherness through 'vocabulary transfer' or just literal translation without changing the co-ordinates, and without taking into account that the parameters of the target culture might differ (widely at times) from one's own, will inevitably lead to misconceptions. We have to accept the fact that the interpretation of 'otherness' will always be subjective, personal and biased - the pictures are painted in the heads of the 'cultural recipients', the L2 users - and they vary; and also the integration of so-called *objective facts* will not change this - on the contrary, they will be used for the subjective interpretation of representations of the target culture.

To reach a more *realistic* and *true* picture of the target culture (still personal, subjective and biased as it may be) the learners will have to apply *specific (inter)cultural strategies* in order to maximise standpoints. Only if a variety of parameters is used, can a more comprehensive view, one that goes beyond first or second sight interpretation be reached. The following intends to identify and to describe some practical strategies, 'didactic tools', so to speak, that might make some contributions to applying intercultural approaches in language teaching.

The first encounter with a foreign culture frequently comes through textbooks or other didactic materials. In the minds of the learners the photographs and pictures presented there, the information about institutions, customs and every day life included contribute to the illusion of a more or less 'complete' and 'relevant' representation of the target culture. Thus, Austria for instance, is frequently *presented* as a German speaking country with some linguistic peculiarities, environmentally friendly, slightly conservative and traditional, Mozart, Sound-of-Music, Alps; sometimes the mention of ski world champions, of mountain bike tracks or other trendy forms of sport leaves the impression of the country as an ideal spare time resort for teens and twens; in other cases it is the great historical past that Austria still stands for today.

No matter which angle is chosen, no matter from which point of view Austria is presented, in all the cases above *answers* are given:

• answers to questions that are not usually asked by the learners themselves;
• answers that prompt *the* or *a* true representation of the target culture;

because of the 'natural authority' of textbooks and textbook authors respectively in all fields of language learning: grammar rules and vocabulary explanations have to be 'correct' and 'true'. This is what the learners must be able to rely on. In the case of intercultural learning, however, this 'reference-book-quality' does not resemble an adequate approach: authors' *opinions* might easily be (mis)taken as *facts*, and the manipulative character of any kind of pre-selection is not (always) made transparent (enough). Instead of a simple 'answer take-over' we would like to suggest the following three principles of awareness raising:

## 1. 'The Art of Questioning'

To see cultural phenomena within *their* own cultural contexts is not always an easy task, partly due to a lack of exposure, partly due to deficits in the availability and relevance of materials. It is suggested therefore that one sensitises oneself by training the *'art of asking the right questions'* in one's own cultural environment. Not just because one's own cultural environment is always 'abundantly' at hand, but because we start from the assumption that cultural (i.e. intercultural, interpretational) skills are not linked to a specific geographical region, country or area. They rather resemble meta-skills and transferable mental attitudes.

### 1.a 'Own and Foreign'

The example below makes use of both knowledge about own and hypotheses about foreign cultures. In the following sequence of activities the techniques of *asking - verifying - questioning* are used.

Topic: 'Foreigners'

Why do foreigners come to, or stay in, a country?

The learners are involved in a constant mutual process of finding questions, looking for answers, verifying hypotheses about own and target country phenomena. The search for sources of information is part of the learning process as well as sensitising oneself, asking whether the kind of questions asked with regard to one's own country would also apply to target culture problems.

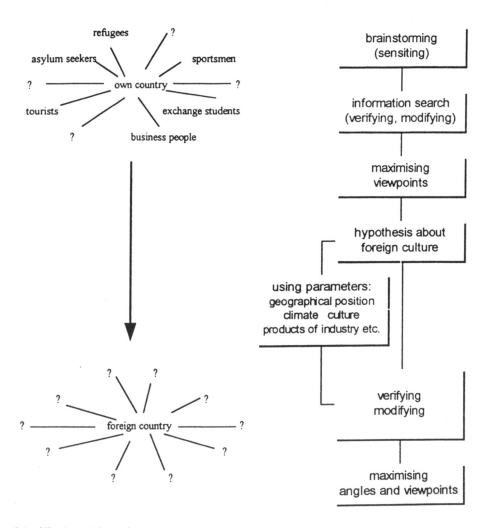

## 1.b 'Ends or Means'

Giving priority to questions and to awareness raising instead of mere facts and figures or someone else's (usually textbook authors') opinions, the value and function of information as such turns from an end in itself to a means, *a tool*. Information search is just one of the techniques, building a hypothesis, finding reasons or certain hints or a basis for this, is another.

Thus, learning a foreign language and trying to *understand* foreign cultures means leaving the classroom situation; external sources and activities outside are integrated and networked into a comprehensive intercultural learning method. The conception of a foreign country does not remain static but undergoes constant changes in a dynamic process. The picture is and has to remain unbalanced and unstable. Opposite to the above mentioned principle of 'answer-takeovers' this approach aims at frequent and critical revision of the learners' interpretation of L2 culture.

### 1.c 'Question the Usual'

By asking (the right) questions the concepts behind the words can be lit up, one's own cultural phenomena are analysed and explained, sometimes divided into its constituents. The learners get the chance to learn about and be made aware of *the complexity of the usual and the commonplace* of their own cultural environment which is a precondition and requirement for asking relevant question about the target culture. Usually, concepts of life, routines of one's own culture are taken for granted, used in a holistic way, 'automatically' based on a (subconsciously accepted) system of co-ordinates. To *identify* these co-ordinates and to *sensitise* for the existence of a system, a framework is needed within which for instance the words (i.e. notions) 'family' or 'movie' are placed.

From a mere lexical point of view there would be no problem at all in transferring the words 'family' or 'movie' from one language into another. Dictionaries of all languages would give a plain, clear one-word equivalent usually without any further commentary. The concepts behind the words, however, which the members of a certain culture have in mind when using these expressions might vary widely.

Let us take a more concrete example out of everyday school life: the Austrian grading system consists of five symbols, the figures 1 to 5 with the former being the best, the latter the worst mark. In other countries it is the other way round. The 'equation' of grades $2 = 4$ , however, need not always, or at least not automatically be correct. The concepts, the systems, have to be compared as well. Answering questions - or thinking of items like the following will help:

- distribution of and consequences of a certain mark;
- what are marks based on;
- prestige of a certain mark among peers;
- parents' reaction to a certain grading
- etc.

When looking at her school report the Austrian pupil below would have the following on her mind (mostly subconsciously) - outsiders on the other hand would need the following annotations as explanations:

coeducational as are 90% of Austrian schools

20% of Austrian teens have finished such a school; entitles to study at university without further exams

compulsory subject, 6 years, reduction discussed in media

40% of class had "3" no "1"s, some "2"s, 4 failed

five written tests and a series of oral exams

drank alcohol at school outing "celebrating" her birthday

dropped the subject as did 40% of class, her own decision

every second week voluntary spare time activity

21 pupils 16 girls

beginning of nine weeks of holidays in summer

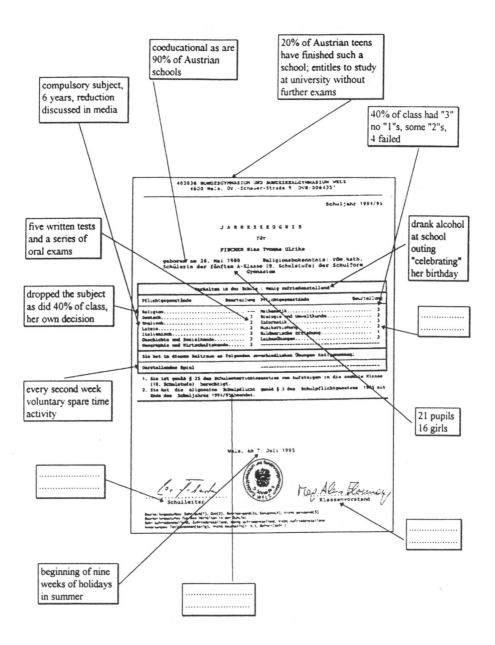

The analysis of *one's own* sociocultural background, the analysis and definition of the parameters forming the framework of a specific culturally relevant situation; for instance, ought to be part of cultural learning, as it resembles an important factor in awareness raising and constitutes the basis for exploring the framework, background and parameters of the target culture. Corresponding questions can be formulated.

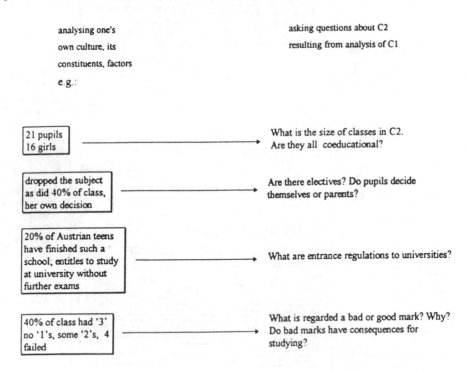

analysing one's own culture, its constituents, factors
e.g.:

asking questions about C2 resulting from analysis of C1

21 pupils
16 girls
→ What is the size of classes in C2. Are they all coeducational?

dropped the subject as did 40% of class, her own decision
→ Are there electives? Do pupils decide themselves or parents?

20% of Austrian teens have finished such a school; entitles to study at university without further exams
→ What are entrance regulations to universities?

40% of class had '3' no '1's, some '2's, 4 failed
→ What is regarded a bad or good mark? Why? Do bad marks have consequences for studying?

## 2.   Doing Puzzles

The strategies suited to gain deeper insight into the characteristics of a foreign culture mentioned so far do not aim at any kind of 'completeness'. On the contrary: it is reminiscent of doing a puzzle: there are always some parts missing, only gradually is the whole picture put together, parts of the whole are completed earlier, some, as it were, will never be completed at all.

Intercultural competence is *partial competence*, allowing illustrative insights. It means equipping learners with techniques and strategies that might be of some help in unexpected, unforeseeable situations. In this context it is not a weakness but a characteristic feature (which is also pointed out clearly in 'ABCD Thesen', a joint effort by experts from the German speaking countries to draw up a list of principles for Landeskunde in language classes). *Deficit awareness,* which in such a scenario will develop simultaneously with growing insight and increasing knowledge, will prevent learners from jumping to hasty conclusions, or passing quick comments just after quick superficial, first sight contacts.

'Doing puzzles' implies *a second principle* as well: working in groups, dividing labour, co-operating, seeking group consensus, trying to get a maximum out of the expertise, skills and approaches of team members. The idea is networking, using a variety of sources and materials, delegating and putting single parts together. Emerging information gaps function as incentives for getting more, and more detailed and varied or specialised information, a starting point for trying to find yet another angle from which to evaluate a certain cultural problem.

Take as an example, a tree, which some see as a symbol for a clean and healthy environment, others just take it as 'raw material' for carpenters or librarians, to yet others it is just an obstruction to street traffic, in barren countries it might be taken as an almost exotic object of desire, a symbol for life, no matter how damaged it might be by acid rain. Interculturally aware learners would have to develop some routine in ascertaining *who* sees *what* in *which* way.

Doing puzzles requires social and interpersonal skills as well as logical thinking, cognitive skills as well as empirical ones, all of which resemble skills upon which intercultural competence is built and which fit very well with a communicative, learner centred approach to language teaching

## 3. Taking photographs and painting pictures

A learner of (inter)cultural competence should be able and trained to do both: take snap shots, reflecting describing and *documenting* reality on the one hand, and taking a painter's approach on the other hand, *interpreting* reality, dealing with feelings and atmosphere, moods and sentiments.

Again, the 'photographer - painter approach' is not only confined to interpreting otherness. One's own surrounding supplies a 'training ground' to sensitise and to develop awareness for these aspects of a certain society as well.

A training tool might be supplied by so-called 'emotional affective filters'. When exploring a foreign or one's own culture, the following puzzle stones, i.e. the following questions might be used to develop and include a range of views:

- What is it that causes frustration to people, individuals or groups, what upsets them and why?
- Can the feelings be transferred to other cultural settings?
- Are there any visions or dreams expressed in letters to the editors of daily papers or weekly magazines?

- Are the people's hopes specific for a certain culture or area, or do people share feelings regardless of their passports or residences?

Information search is expanded by search for feelings and emotions.

The 'painter-photographer awareness' is required when it comes to interpreting objects of modern art, paintings, sculptures. In such abstract areas, independent of specific linguistic or cultural contexts, the specific required skills under discussion are made transparent most effectively. Elements of creativity and of interpretation of artefacts therefore ought to be taken into the standards of language tuition.

## References

Fischer, R. et al. (1990) "Thesen zur Rolle der Landeskunde im Deutschunterricht". *DaF - Mitteilungen* 2, 1991, p. 26.

Fischer, R. (1994) "Curriculare Aspekte der Landeskunde der 90er Jahre". In Report on Workshop 14.

Morgan, J. and Welton, P. (1986) *See what I mean. An Introduction to Visual Communication*. London, New York, Melbourne: Edward Arnold.

Müller, B.-D. (1994)*Wortschatzarbeit und Bedeutungsvermittlung*. München: Langenscheidt.

Neuner, G. (1994) "Aufgaben und Übungsgeschehen im Deutschunterricht". *Fremdsprache Deutsch* 10, pp. 6 - 14.

Report on Workshop 13A/Rapport de l'Atelier 13A *'Language and culture awareness in language teaching (L2 and L1) for the development of learner autonomy (age 11-18)/Sensibilisation à la langue et à la culture dans l'apprentissage/enseignement des langues (L1 et L2) et développement de l'autonomie de l'apprenant (11-18 years).'* Santa Margherita Ligure (Genova/Gênes), Italy/Italie, December/décembre 1993. Doc. CC-LANG (95) Workshop 13A/Atelier 13A. Compiled and edited by/coordonné par F. Palamidesi Cesaretti/N. Galli De'Paratesi.

Rall, M. (1990) "Wo steht die Sonne am Mittag?" *Fremdsprache Deutsch* 3, pp. 24 - 36.

Report on Workshop 14/Bericht über Workshop 14 *'Landeskunde im DaF - Unterricht für Jugendliche und Erwachsene. Regionale Vielfalt am Beispiel Österreichs'*. Rust am Neusiedlersee, Burgenland (Österreich), Mai 1994. Doc. CC-LANG (94) Workshop 14 - revised. Zusammengestellt von W. Hackl.

Sheils, J. (1992) *Communication in the modern languages classroom*. Strasbourg: Council of Europe.

# TRAINING LANGUAGE TEACHERS IN THE PEDAGOGY OF EXCHANGES - TOWARDS THE DEVELOPMENT OF SOCIOCULTURAL COMPETENCE

*Silvia MITTEREGGER, Switzerland*

> L'étranger est en moi,
> donc nous sommes tous des étrangers.
> Si je suis étranger, il n'y a pas d'étrangers.
> *Julia Kristeva (1988: 284)*

> À la limite utopique, tout l'enseignement
> des langues étrangères pourrait être conçu et
> organisé autour, à partir des échanges.
> *René Richterich (1994: 4)*

## Introduction

What can initial and in-service teacher education contribute in the context of school exchanges? It is not difficult to answer this question or to find reasons for the importance of introducing school exchanges into teacher education at a time of new projects in the Council of Europe, or new programmes in the European Union such as Socrates or Comenius.

However, I propose first of all to discuss the question of why the so-called 'pedagogy of exchanges' (Richterich, 1994) has such a marginal place in initial and in-service education of teachers in general and language teachers in particular. I shall use the example of Switzerland as a source of experience and a focus of analysis. On the other hand, using several selected examples of projects in which Switzerland is a partner, I shall show how teachers can gain further training with respect to acquisition or development of their sociocultural competence, through participation in exchange projects. In order to broaden the admittedly restricted horizons of Swiss experience, I shall describe the first steps and experiences of a tri-national research and development project from Council of Europe Workshop 18, in which Norwegian, Portuguese and Swiss participants are working together on the development of modules of in-service teacher education for the 'pedagogy of exchanges'. The concept itself is defined by Richterich (1994: 4) as follows:

"Rappelons que la didactique des langues étrangères a pour objet la transformation des actions d'enseignement (transmettre des savoirs, savoir-faire, savoir-être, savoir-paraître) en actions d'apprentissage (reproduire, exploiter, adapter, inventer des savoirs, savoir-faire, savoir-apprendre, savoir-être, savoir-paraître). Alors que la pédagogie des langues étrangères s'efforce de définir le sens, la valeur, la finalité, les conditions de réalisation des relations entre enseignants et apprenants dans le processus de cette transformation. C'est pourquoi il me paraît plus adéquat d'utiliser le terme de pédagogie dans les échanges plutôt que celui de didactique."

## A first insight from the Swiss perspective

Because of the specific language situation - a multilingual and multicultural country - linguistic and cultural bridge building in general, and school exchanges in particular, has always had a special significance in Switzerland, for state and language policy reasons. It is seen in politics, education and research as well as in the practice of schooling as a contribution to mutual comprehension between the different language groups and to the maintenance of the unity of the country. Furthermore it is considered to be an important element in the reform of language teaching in the form in which this has taken in Switzerland since the 1980s.

If one considers the practice of exchange in the last ten years, it is easy to see that the aims and contents of exchange projects are usually linked to foreign language teaching and learning. The reasons for this are not only of a linguistic policy kind. They are related among other things to the reasoning by which pupil and teacher exchanges are recognised and encouraged in educational institutions in Switzerland. These are in turn important for teachers who wish to become involved with exchange projects because they give them the institutional legitimation which allows a project of this kind to be realised.

The first official text of the Schweizerische Konferenz der kantonalen Erziehungsdirektoren (EDK) concerning exchanges arose in the context of the reform and introduction of teaching of the country's second language at primary level. It is also clear that the idea of exchanges is linked with the reform of language teaching from the example of a further significant text from the EDK in the context of the definition of aims and methods for teaching the second language. In this text, general pedagogical principles are formulated as well as subject-specific learning objectives:

> "The learning objectives of foreign language teaching should not be determined only according to subject-specific perspectives (....) It is important that pupils learn a foreign language, but it is even more important that they learn to act independently, to take responsibility and to work together with other people."
> (EDK, 1987: 21)

In addition it was recommended that, in the general educational aims of foreign language teaching, pupils should develop a positive attitude to multilingualism in general and in Switzerland in particular, should understand and be able to relate to people who speak another language, should acquire insights into other language areas and should demonstrate understanding for the specificity of other language groups.

As already mentioned, educational exchanges were, until recently, strongly orientated to foreign languages and followed rather conventional lines with respect to methodology. However, as a result of the introduction of new methods of teaching and learning in our schools, in particular of open learning forms such as project work, the practice of exchanges has also changed radically. Thus today, as well as justifications on language policy and citizenship grounds, increasing emphasis is given to general pedagogical aspects such as participation and partnership learning and teaching, teacher-pupil relationships, co-operation between organising school and parents, interdisciplinarity, teamwork among teachers, the development of an understanding of sociocultural relationships through personal experience, and so on. It is also true that school pupils and apprentices are now much more interested in international exchange opportunities. This is connected with factors such as the opening up of Central and Eastern Europe, the new trends in intercultural learning, the North-South dialogue, peace education, the European dimension in school and much more, and this in turn also means that the issue of exchanges is in constant flux with respect to contents, aims and methods.

The need for initial and in-service training for teachers with respect to the realisation of these aims is however not mentioned in the official texts. Furthermore, if one considers the numerous opportunities for teacher training continually offered by various public and private institutions, it is striking that there are very few opportunities for further training in the pedagogy of exchanges. There are various reasons for this. Organisers of exchanges were hitherto often isolated in their schools, since pupil and teacher exchange was considered the business of the foreign language teacher. In Switzerland it is clear that exchange projects have been run for years by the same individuals, who have been trained as it were 'on the job' in a process of self-education. Although the pedagogical value of the exchange is not questioned, the exchange of pupils and teachers is still considered by the educational authorities to be a marginal phenomenon which only affects a few teaching staff. So it appears to those responsible for initial and in-service training that the question of the pedagogy of exchanges is not relevant enough to merit specific courses being developed.

## A pilot project: teacher and pupil exchange as a new dimension of in-service teacher training

It has always been acknowledged that real-life cultural exchange and partnership co-operation, such as the pedagogy of exchanges is assumed to be, is of exceptional pedagogical value, since such encounters involve experiential learning. It is however too little known that from a pedagogical and psychological perspective, such encounters are in every respect complex experiences not only for young people but also for adults. An exchange often involves the first closely experienced engagement with 'the other', with another language and culture, with other ways of life, other social structures and value systems. The exchange must therefore be seen and developed as a multi-layered learning process, which like every engagement with the new and unknown, first makes one insecure and anxious because  - especially for teaching staff  - it calls everything into question.

Because of this awareness that the success or failure of programmes of exchange and encounter is directly dependent on how the organising teaching staff acquire access to the other language and cultural arena, a pilot project was begun by the Nordwestschweizerischen Erziehungsdirektorenkonferenz in co-operation with the Academies of Strasbourg and Besançon in the context of the introduction of the early learning of foreign languages.  The project was structured as follows:

---

Opening seminar                                             (2 days)
- first contacts between teaching staff, 'partner fair'
- creation of the 'exchange partners'
- introduction to the pedagogy of exchanges
- planning of the individual exchange projects

Staff exchange                                              (2 x 1 week)
- one week each observing in the partner school

Interim seminar                                             (1 day)
- evaluation of the teacher exchanges
- ideas swap-shop with respect to pupil exchanges

Pupil exchanges                                             (2 x 1 week)
- the participating teachers decide form,
  content and exact length

Concluding seminar                                          (1 day)
- evaluation of the projects
- planning for the continuation of the exchanges or
  partnership work

---

The basic idea was that for the participating teachers their own experience of cultural differences and partnership co-operation would be far more efficient and meaningful as a form of in-service training in the pedagogy of exchanges than traditional courses. Furthermore the organisers started from the belief that such training is only meaningful if teachers work within an administrative and financial framework which is guaranteed by the responsible institutions.  On the other hand they must have as much freedom as possible in the formulation of the aims of the exchange and in the structuring of the teaching methods in the exchange projects (Racine, 1991).

The programme lasts a whole school year so that the teachers have enough time to build up the project together. The participating schools also agree to remain in contact with their partner schools beyond the one year of the project in order to ensure continuity. The exchange teachers can count on continuing expert advice thanks to three seminars and regular contacts with local people responsible for exchanges and with a central expert institution. The three seminars also serve from the point of view of the participating teachers as an important point for exchange of experience and 'reflexive analysis' - a kind of formative evaluation - and this allows them to see their own projects in another light, to change them and develop them further.

The heart of the project for the participating teachers is without doubt the opportunity to put themselves for a week in the place of a learner, i.e. the pupil who will later take part in the class exchange, who has to come to terms with another linguistic and cultural environment. The exchange of teachers which follows the opening seminar allows them to submerge themselves in the culture of the other language area, to get to know another school system, the partner school, school staff and classes, and also to improve their own linguistic skills. The participating pupils and parents thus get to know the partner teacher personally and are brought into the project work from the beginning, taking a more motivated role in the exchange which follows.

This programme has been evaluated annually since its inception. What is particularly revealing is how the participating teachers evaluate the exchange from their own perspective. I shall attempt to analyses here, by the use of quotations from teachers, what changes the project has created in the teachers and how they develop their sociocultural competence. These are extracts of particular relevance which represent the general tendencies in the teachers' responses.

### The teacher exchange

'Engaging with and experiencing others and with otherness, is crucial.'
'La période d'assistanat me paraît de la plus haute importance. Il s'agissait de découvrir une vie scolaire différente et de construire des liens de confiance.'

It seems to be clear that the teacher exchange is of crucial importance for participating teachers because it allows them to develop an understanding of the other school system and the value system within it through their taking the role of an observer in their partner teacher's school. This facilitates a comparison with their own system and also with their own way of teaching. On the other hand they also have the opportunity - and this seems to be even more important from the point of view of efficiency - to teach in the partnership class and thus to adapt to a new school environment, either independently or in co-operation with their exchange partner.

The evaluation of approximately sixty exchange projects from the last five years has shown that the biggest problems and conflicts have been during the final phase, i.e. during and after the exchanges of pupils, whereas during the teacher exchanges there have been hardly any problems of significance. This is linked to several factors, but is certainly related to the fact that pupil exchanges are experienced by many teachers as stressful, demanding much psychological and physical effort. The pressure under which many teachers find themselves is also connected to the high expectations which pupils, parents, head teachers and school authorities and also the teachers themselves have of the pupil exchanges.

## Teachers in their professional and social environment

### School systems

> 'La rencontre culturelle par l'intermédiaire de la connaissance des institutions me semble centrale.'
> 'Ce sont les aspects relationnels et de différence de culture qui m'ont le plus marqué.

The experience of teacher and pupil exchanges contains of course many risks, not least because the sociocultural and professional environment is fundamentally altered for the exchange teacher. The personal experience of fundamentally different beliefs about what the educational aims of the school are, and what the means are with which it seeks to realise them, what the role of the teacher is with respect to school authorities, head teacher, teacher colleagues, parents and pupils, within what framework a teacher in another country operates, and so on, forces the teacher to make comparisons with their own professional and social environment. This experience can be deeply disturbing and call into question everything hitherto known and familiar. It can however also strengthen one's conviction that one's own values and school system are right. Other teachers seize this experience as an opportunity to transfer, in the spirit of the true exchange, things which are particularly interesting or sensible into their own school environment, or to work in co-operation with their partner teacher on matters of common interest.

The complex of issues in the different school systems justifies the existence of the opening seminar described above because these complexities are explained and discussed in detail. Moreover, head teachers are also always invited to this event, and as a consequence of this, and of the fact that they are only present in the schools for a limited period and thus have a 'special status' as guests, the exchange teachers usually find the atmosphere in the partner school to be friendly and stimulating.

### Teacher and pupil exchange as professional enrichment

> 'The project was one of the best things I have ever done. It gave me a new motivation which had an effect on my whole school life.'

Teachers emphasise again and again how positively participation in such a project affects them on a general personal or private level. At the same time it is noticeable that developments in their expertise or their foreign language capacity are felt to be far less important.

> 'There were teachers who were prepared to open their classrooms and to allow the guests an insight into the school.'
> 'My colleagues admire my work.'
> 'The reactions of colleagues were varied, including on the one hand pleasure and support and on the other, envy and resentment. Colleagues who are afraid of such activities don't want to be given such examples to follow.'

The question of their own well-being also depends, so the teachers emphasise themselves, on the satisfaction which the exchange gives the teacher with respect to their role in their own school and social context. The exchange project and the persons involved are often seen as something special, as carriers of a positive idea, as fighting for something good. It is understandable that this can provoke envy and resentment among colleagues, and it is therefore not surprising that in many reports the lack of co-operation with one's own colleagues is mentioned as one of the negative elements of the exchange project.

On the other hand it is frequently evident how positively the project affects team work in one's own school. The partnership thinking which affects the co-operation with the partner school creates direct consequences for the functioning of one's own school and also gives particular value in their own school to the role of the teacher responsible for the exchange.

*School head teachers, authorities and the general public*

> 'I am really enthusiastic about the opportunities of the exchange. It has given me the courage to try similar activities and to represent them in the community.'
> 'La direction de l'établissement a donné carte blanche pour toute initiative dans le cadre de l'échange.'
> 'Le maire a offert le pot de bienvenue.'

These quotations reveal, even though in a rather veiled way, that the relationship of the teacher involved in the exchange to those above them changes for the better as a consequence of the project. It is frequently noticeable how particularly active teachers who involve head teachers and school authorities in the exchange, gain a certain confidence on a personal, social and professional level. The foreign language and international dimension also gives them a certain authority thanks to which they can excel within their own school or community. It is also interesting in this context that many teachers remark that it was through the administrative and organisational preparations for the exchange that they got to know the structures of their own educational administration and to obtain results from head teachers and school authorities. Furthermore it is also evident that many teachers become involved in public affairs, contacts with the local press, radio and television and thus make their work and that of their colleagues better known outside the school. Teachers often remark that they develop skills which they had not expected of themselves.

## The teacher-pupil relationship

'The exchange helped to create a positive relationship between me as teacher and my pupils, and to develop co-operative work with my colleagues.'

Almost all exchange reports emphasise the positive effects which the exchange brings to the teacher-pupil relationship. This is doubtless connected with the fact that the idea of the partnership does not just determine the teacher-teacher relationship but also that between teacher and pupils and teacher and parents. However some cases have been observed where the exchange has been the catalyst in the development of deep-seated differences between teacher and pupils. Questions to the teachers involved suggest that the teacher responsible for the exchange is also seen as a learner, at least partially, (e.g. because it is the first time they are organising an exchange or because they do not speak the foreign language well) and this can make the teacher insecure and robs them of the authority which is fundamental for their definition of their role as teacher.

## Co-operation with parents

'Les parents d'élèves ont été des partenaires compréhensifs et coopératifs.'
'There were similar anxieties as with the children.'
'The parents saw the enthusiasm of their children and could only respond positively.'

The idea of partnership which thanks to the exchange can develop with parents is a further constant feature in the evaluation of exchange projects. This aspect is however perceived in a variety of ways, and is also related to the degree to which or the ways in which co-operation with parents above and beyond the exchange is already firmly anchored in the respective country. That this dimension can also have a positive effect on the development of teachers' sociocultural competence is shown by the fact that its importance is recognised by those teachers who had hitherto not been involved in this kind of constructive, partnership co-operation. This form of co-operation, which opens the school to the surrounding society, necessarily changes the teacher-parent relationship since the teacher is obliged to rely upon parental co-operation, for example in the case of pupil exchanges with accommodation in host families where the support of the parents is vital.

This attempt at systematising and analysis naturally only illuminates a small part of what is involved in the exchange programmes for teachers and pupils described here. The impressive variety of ideas and activities scarcely allows a full description of the programme, and many examples of projects can be found in the journal *Trait d'union* published by *ch* Jugendaustausch, Soluthurn.

**The R&D Project 'Training Language Teachers for a Multicultural Europe through the *Pédagogie des échanges*': towards a methodology**

New-style Workshop 18A took place in Lillehammer, Norway, in October 1995. It dealt with the role of school exchanges and school partnerships in the context of teaching and learning foreign languages.

Approximately 50 participants from 32 countries were in six project groups dealing with different aspects of the theme. Two trends became evident: on the one hand considerable interest in the question of formulating pedagogical guidelines and the development of practical help with respect to the organisation and the structuring of the content of exchanges; on the other hand, there was the question of the initial and in-service training of teachers and head teachers with respect to the exchange.

The international context made possible by the new-style workshops of the Council of Europe is particularly stimulating when the topic is the realisation of projects on the 'pedagogy of the exchange' and offers an appropriate framework for co-operation with partners from other institutional, sociocultural and professional backgrounds.

Like the function of the teacher exchanges described above, such an occasion is on the one hand a multinational and therefore complex opportunity for in-service training on professional issues, which facilitates the confrontation with other ways of working, other contextual conditions, and other educational aims. On the other hand, the workshop provides for educational professionals concerned with exchanges, an ideal environment for personal concrete experience of the dynamics of intercultural encounters, for testing one's own capacity to communicate and negotiate, and for the confrontation with the question of one's own linguistic and professional knowledge, and of one's own sociocultural competences. If one also considers the projects resulting from the Workshop in the area of teacher initial and in-service training, then it is easy to defend the view that such meetings are absolutely necessary for the successful completion of projects (see also Aede/Grefes 1993; Heitz, 1994; Wengler,1995; Aavv, in press).

**A practical and empirical approach: an initial and in-service project on the pedagogy of the exchange**

There are a growing number of initial and in-service courses on the pedagogy of the exchange and an increasing need by teachers, both in initial training and already in the profession, for information, concrete help and the opportunity for more in-depth analysis of the topic. There is also a need to develop an appropriate methodology. This was the starting point for one of the groups not simply to reflect on theoretical issues but rather to develop practical ideas and proposals in their respective countries, and to test their ideas in the professional environment of initial and in-service teacher training.

The group formulated its general project aims independently of the different national contexts:

- the development and implementation of in-service modules which motivate, sensitise and give the skills of producing projects to foreign language teachers with respect to the pedagogy of the exchange.

The group's main purpose was to produce an inventory of courses in the participating countries and a regular exchange of information, and then on this basis to develop and implement modules, at a national and regional level. The group was not able to proceed to the next stage of further international training projects because of lack of time.

## Co-operation and networking in the R&D project: experiences and perspectives

First a very banal finding: the implementation of inter-regional and international projects whether in the area of teacher and pupil exchanges or in teacher training - presupposes that there will be people who can agree on project aims, contents and methods, and who have at their disposal the necessary time and sufficient motivation needed to implement such projects. Although this may seem banal. these pre-conditions are not always easy to establish. Usually there has to be some external cause or occasion which brings people together so that such affinities can crystallise. Workshop 18 provided such an opportunity to develop informal networks of people at many different levels who shared similar tendencies and interests. In spite of the informal nature of these mini-networks, the co-operation was successful because of these pre-conditions: openness and flexibility, consistency and commitment, motivation and capacity for communication. We shall only note in passing that other significant factors do not necessarily disappear because of the informality of such networks, for example disposable time, financial means and institutional support.

### *The example of Norway: the creation of a national network*

The fact that there were three participants from different parts of Norway in the group which took the theme of 'Training Language Teachers for a Multicultural Europe through the 'Pédagogie des échanges' led not only to the planned international network but also to a national network on an inter-regional basis.

Due to strong motivation on the part of the various people there was at national level:

- regular exchange of ideas, materials and experience;
- mutual professional support and concrete co-operation, for example in the form of invitation lectures in the respective institutions (teacher training institutions, school-based in-service training, etc.) expertise and consultation in the implementation of projects etc;
- the integration of the 'Pédagogie des échanges' in the training courses organised by the members of the group.

*The example of Switzerland: 'expert-networks'*

Proposals and implementations were developed in Switzerland in ways similar to those in Norway. In addition to pre-existing projects and courses, new initial and in-service courses were tested in Switzerland in the area of the basic training of foreign language teachers and with respect to the in-service training of teachers at all levels and types of school throughout Switzerland, with the participation of speakers from Workshop 18A. 'Networking' meant in this case, that the professional know-how of various participants in the Workshop could be used in the Swiss context too.

## Conclusion

The examples of pragmatic, uncomplicated co-operation demonstrate how experience which usually remains isolated can be useful to others, and how through mutual support new projects can be started. In the final analysis, the 'Pédagogie des échanges' acquires more impetus through interregional co-operation and - as our reported experience has shown - has a better chance of implementation.

It remains to hope that the materials and proposals which have arisen from this will be usable in the same way by a wider circle of teachers and trainers throughout Europe who have an interest in the 'Pédagogie des échanges'

## References

Aavv, in press, *Repères pour la formation des enseignants à la pédagogie des échanges.* Strasbourg: Council of Europe.

Aede/Grefes, (1993) *La pédagogie des échanges - Buts et moyens de la formation des enseignants.* Strasbourg: Council of Europe.

Heitz, E. (1994) "Pour un parcours individuel de formation aux échanges scolaires". In Alix C. & Bertrand G. (eds.) *Pour une pédagogie des échanges.* Special issue of *Le français dans le monde.* Feb-March, pp. 166-171.

Kristeva, J. (1988) *Etrangers à nous-mêmes* Paris: Fayard.

Racine, J. (1991) "Die Pilotprojekte: SchülerInnen- und LehrerInnenaustausch in der Praxis. Nordschweizerische Erziehungsdirektorenkonferenz" (ed) *Doppelpunkt,* 16, pp. 4 & ff

Richterich, R. (1994) "Echange=change. Jalons pour une pédagogie du changement". In *ch* Stiftung (ed.) *Vademecum* Soluthurn: *ch*Stiftung.

Schweizerische Konferenz der Kantonalen Erziehungs-Direktoren (EDK) (1987) *Herausforderung Schweiz. Materialien zur Förderung des Unterrichts in den Landessprachen* Bern: EDK.

Wengler, A. (ed.) (1995) *Echanges scolaire multilatéraux et interculturels,* Luxembourg: Ministère de l'éducation nationale

# SOCIOCULTURAL COMPETENCE IN A 'LEARNING TO LEARN' CONTEXT

*Anne-Brit FENNER, Norway*

## Background

This article will present some aspects of a project on cultural competence in a group of 14 year-old Norwegian learners of English. The main aim of the project was to increase their sociocultural competence. The classroom experiment was based on learner autonomy.

The framework of the project was part of the language programme administered by the Council of Europe started at Workshop 13A in 1993 and finished at Workshop 13B in 1996 but the duration of the experimentation phase in the classroom was only one school year. The title of the project as presented in a report to the Council of Europe was 'Awareness of Language, Culture and Learning as Means towards Learner Autonomy'.

The classroom project consisted of several sub-projects. The school year was divided into periods of work of varying duration, followed by evaluation by the learners as well as by the teacher. Both process and products were evaluated. In this article only two of the sub-projects that the learners planned and carried out, have been chosen in order to present specific aspects of cultural competence. The projects were carried out in different ways, but self-directed learning was common to them all, as was the aim of improving the learners' sociocultural competence.

Before describing the classroom project itself, I want first to define learner autonomy, as this was the setting in which the project was carried out. Self-directed learning was also an inherent part of the classroom procedures during the project period. Secondly, I shall explain how the term culture was understood by the learners, as they chose most of the initial content of the whole project.

## Learner Autonomy

According to Holec's definition (1979:3), autonomy is 'the ability to take charge of one's own learning', which he defines as

to have, and to hold, the responsibility for all the decisions concerning all aspects of this learning, ie:

- determining the objectives;
- defining the contents;
- selecting methods and techniques to be used...;
- evaluating what has been acquired.

Through a systematic progression of increasing the amount of responsibility given to each learner, the focus in the classroom to be described here had been gradually changed from teaching to learning during the year preceding the project. The learners' choice of material and approach had been important aspects of the learning process. In the present Norwegian national curriculum (Mønsterplanen - 87) the overall aim of foreign language learning is communicative competence, but the term is not made specific, and the didactic freedom of teacher and learners is very wide. This does not, however, mean that this freedom is explored in most Norwegian foreign language classrooms.

In order to preserve the responsibility that the learners had been accustomed to, they had in most sub-projects the freedom to choose or influence the following aspects of the learning process:

- the topic;
- some or all of the material;
- whether to work in groups, in pairs or individually;
- the approach;
- the form of 'publication' or presentation;
- evaluation of the process, product and what had been learnt.

In *Learner Autonomy: Definitions, Issues and Problems*, Little (1991: 7) states that:

> "the learner generates his own purpose for learning; in pursuit of those purposes he determines not only the content of learning but the way in which learning will take place... In other words, the curriculum now comes from within the learner, as a product of his past experience and present and future needs."

I believe that in any classroom situation the learner, as a matter of course, is in control of the way in which his *learning* takes place, the teacher can only decide in what way the *teaching* will take place. But what is specific to a learning-to-learn situation, is that both teacher and learner are aware of this fact and act accordingly. It is, however, specific to self-directed learning that the curriculum comes from within the learner. In this project on cultural competence, this fact caused a problem. I want to call it a dilemma of choice, and it can be argued as follows.

When the learner chooses his own curriculum, this curriculum becomes a product of his past experience. His background is one determining factor in his choice, part of what Bourdieu calls *habitus*. Left with a completely free choice, the young learner will choose within his own scope. Some learners are in possession of great 'culture capital', others have limited resources. (Bourdieu, 1993) After several years of letting learners choose their learning material, I now see it as essential for the teacher to assist learners in their choice of material in order to extend their existing knowledge. Working with the concept of cultural competence, young learners should have the opportunity to lift their eyes beyond their own narcissist youth culture and beyond a solely utilitarian view of language and culture. Fully aware of the danger of an instrumentalist approach, certain limits were put on the learners' choice of material.

## Culture

Most Norwegian children are highly motivated to learn English. They realise that it is essential for people who live in a small country to communicate with others. Many young people travel abroad. English is also part of their everyday lives through television, films and computers[1]. This is also true for the not-so-clever pupils, who, perhaps, watch more video films without subtitles than many of the so-called clever children. In Norway, English is becoming a second language more than a foreign language.

As their linguistic competence is partly achieved through encountering authentic language in an out-of-school context, their knowledge of American and British culture is also considerable, at least within certain fields of knowledge. This is true, for instance, of pop-music and the media world - youth culture in general. The learners are, however, not always aware of their cultural competence, perhaps because teachers show little interest in the learners' private worlds outside school where such competence is achieved. It may also be that the learners themselves consider their private lives to be of little consequence to the teachers and to what happens in the English lessons. Their personal knowledge is often considered to be different from, and irrelevant to, school knowledge. Much could be gained if the knowledge and competence obtained outside school were considered part of their language and culture competence, and given scope to develop further inside the classroom. (Illich, 1979)

It was only natural that, in a classroom where the learners were used to making decisions about their own learning material and approach, they should have a say in planning the project work on cultural competence. I decided to start with learners' associations with the word 'culture'. This would provide both me and the learners themselves with information about their understanding of the term. The following list was supplied by learners in answer to the question, 'What do you understand by the word "culture" ?':

---

[1]     In Norway, films are subtitled and not dubbed. As the majority of films are American or English, this constitutes an important exposure to the target language which most other European nationals do not have.

| - national costumes | - clothes |
|---|---|
| - language | - traditions |
| - Sami people, Indians | - transport |
| - history | - paintings |
| - food | - behaviour |
| - museums | - looks |
| - hobbies | - architecture |
| - religion | - literature |
| - music | - history of writing |
| - nature | - newspapers |

Such an extensive list seemed a good starting point for work on cultural competence. The learners had come up with a wide range of associations and the work could proceed from their existing knowledge in almost any direction they chose. Their answers were interesting as their associations were not only connected with everyday experience. The fact that some of them thought of language as culture, indicated that they had a certain understanding of culture which they had not gained from the textbook. Associations with ethnic groups were surprising as were architecture, painting and literature, the more traditional definition of culture as fine art. This wide scope of associations would probably not have been the result if we had previously worked with a traditional foreign language textbook without authentic texts. When we *had* used a textbook, it was one with few of the traditional role-plays and information-gap exercises inherent in the 'communicative competence' type textbook. Instead we had used a lot of authentic material supplied by the learners and the teacher, and the learners had gained a fairly wide reading experience.

## Planning the projects

All the projects were based on the belief that:

- culture and language are inter-related;
- this inter-relationship can only be found in authentic material;
- literature is the personal voice of a culture;
- language learning is a creative and personal process;
- language learning is negotiating meaning with people or with texts;
- the quality of texts influences the quality of learning;
- through understanding the foreign culture, one gains a deeper understanding of one's own.

These beliefs were based on psychology of learning, cultural studies, literary theory, linguistic theory in addition to classroom experience and constituted the foundation of the whole classroom project from the teacher's point of view.

The immediate consequences of such beliefs were that in the classroom emphasis was put on gaining cultural competence through interpreting meaning of language as cultural artefact, not on learning *about* culture. Furthermore, that written and oral authentic texts were used as much as possible. We focused upon extensive reading of literary texts and extensive writing, using model texts. Throughout the project year, emphasis was put on a wide range of personal interpretation of tasks and texts. The list of associations that the pupils had come up with was used for each new planning phase.

One aspect of learner autonomy is that it is not possible for the teacher to plan everything in advance. A task that is finished will open up for new planning, a new need for learning as a result of reflection on the previous task. In this case it was important that the choices were made in collaboration with the pupils, or by them alone.

What I have previously termed the "dilemma of choice" prompted a discussion with the learners in which it was agreed that the class would work on a common topic or even the same material for some of the sub-projects, but the way they planned and carried out the work, was up to them.

For each new task there was a period of planning. In some cases the planning would be in groups, in other cases it would be done individually. Group planning through negotiation is an important part of communicative experience, perhaps the best opportunity in the classroom for authentic conversation. Planning a project involves having to express opinions, agree and disagree, negotiate and interpret, all of which are essential in the development of communicative competence. The next step, informing the teacher of what has been planned, means reflecting on the choices made. Having to give reasons and defending choices, from the point of view of personal learning, is part of developing learning awareness and meta-cognition. The planning would then be followed by a work period which in some cases would be evaluated in the process. When the work was done, ending in some kind of product, a period of self-evaluation and evaluation by the teacher would complete the task.

This process was the main framework of the sub-projects and tasks that were undertaken during the year. In the next part of the article two of the sub-projects will be presented in order to show different aspects of cultural competence.


**The Industrial Revolution**

At the beginning of the year the learners included history in their associations with the word culture. The class was studying the Industrial Revolution in their history lessons, and it seemed natural to do the same topic in the English lessons as the history books deal with the revolution in Britain and not in Norway. Here was an opportunity for the learners to interact with the historical texts in order to understand a culture twice removed, a foreign culture and a distant historical period.

The learning-to-learn aspect should hopefully make it possible for the learners to approach authentic material without having it digested for them and passed on by the teacher, thus having a chance to interpret the historical events directly. Again, it was important that we did not just read *about* the revolution, but that we studied the self-expression of the event if possible. In Unwin's *Question of Evidence: Britain since 1700*, I found authentic source material; cartoons from the 18th century, letters, court hearings and witness reports from factory owners and workers, especially children. The only text we used from a foreign language textbook, was one about chimney-sweepers. Using different authentic texts is an attempt at making the learners realise that meeting a foreign culture is not facing one true and indisputable reality, but various webs that need interpretation before each learner can create his or her own meaning.

Learners were given all these texts, told to choose two and then give reasons for their choices. I also wanted to use a few literary texts but realised that they would be difficult for the age-group. We read William Blake's *The Chimney Sweeper* from *Songs of Innocence and of Experience*. The class had, in the previous year written some poetry themselves, and did not regard poetry in itself as difficult. In their history books they had read a Norwegian version of Elizabeth Barrett Browning's *The Cry of the Children*. Only a few stanzas had been rewritten. We decided to approach this extensive and rather difficult poem as an experiment in dealing with complicated authentic texts. In this part of the project the learners were given little choice.

They read and then tried to translate the abbreviated Norwegian version into English. Many learners take a long time to really comprehend that there is not necessarily one English word that corresponds with every Norwegian word. Even where there seems to be a direct translation, the word might carry a culturally different connotation. A house in Norwegian, (hus) is, for instance, not like an English house. The discovery of the relationship between languages thus becomes an aspect of cultural as well as linguistic competence. Translation sometimes speeds up this process of discovery.

They struggled hard with the Norwegian version, and were given the opportunity to translate as many stanzas as they wanted. The task was not product-oriented, it was an attempt at a strategy which would enable them to understand a difficult authentic text. Then they read the original in English. By this time the learners were aware of most of the difficult words they had struggled with, and were very keen to find out how Elizabeth Barrett Browning had 'solved the problem'. The result was that even the weakest learners were eager to read and to understand what, at the beginning, was considered a far too difficult text for this age-group. It had now become a text each of them personally had struggled to 'create'. This part of the classroom experiment proved that the way in which an authentic text is approached often determines how the learners cope with it, rather than the language level. It is also a means of meeting the foreign culture through a text and not reading it primarily to learn new vocabulary.

The next part of the project was the learners' own language production. Integrating the skills was part of the classroom procedure and so they had to choose what type of written work they wanted to do. This was a topic for classroom negotiation, and learners came up with the following types of texts that they could write:

- a government complaint;
- an article;
- a poem;
- a factory-worker's diary;
- the diary of a chimney-sweeper;
- a story;
- a letter to the editor of a newspaper;
- an interview.

Any of these tasks would put learners in a situation where they would have to write in a foreign language about a distant historical situation as something personally felt. This was a fairly complex situation to find themselves in, but a very useful one when working with cultural competence.

The result of their written work was good. They had been inspired by the literary models; five pupils wrote poems about the topic. They had, to a certain extent, managed to interact with the historical narrative, and create their own narratives in the foreign language. The industrial revolution makes an impression on this age-group because of the way children suffered. They easily identify with the feeling of injustice.

I want to include one poem in this report to show an example of the work done. Through the writing process minor linguistic corrections have been made, and the rhythm has been adjusted in a few places.

THE INDUSTRIAL REVOLUTION

Manchester was a nice little town,
And the population was small.
People lived on their own,
With more than enough space for all.

Suddenly a great revolution,
The town grew more and more.
Certain was the conclusion:
It wasn't the same as before.

The city was full of sewage,
Along the road there were plenty of pipes.
Nasty and great was the damage;
You could see in the air the black stripes.

Children had none of their childhood.
In the darkest mines and factories,
They had to work more than they should.
Under pressure they swept narrow chimneys.

Slowly there were new rules.
Trade unions came in a crowd.
The workers got better tools.
Factory children were not allowed.

Now most of the countries have industry,
In a new and more cunning way.
Cleaned is the waste from the factory,
And we try to get better every day.
(Henriette Lorentz)

The poem shows a good understanding of the historical situation. She describes the almost pastoral scene before the revolution, and then the change as a violent transformation. By contrasting the situation before and after, she conveys an insight into the Romantic portrayal of the period. There is also epic movement in the poem. The finishing stanza indicates her ability to generalise the problem of pollution at the time of the industrial revolution and make it a modern problem. At the end she conveys the optimism of an adolescent who is involved in problems of her own time and feels an urge to solve them.

I find this poem an interesting result of the classroom work on the industrial revolution. Here is a learner who employs the knowledge she has gained in her history lessons and in her English lessons. The personal voice of the authentic material used in English is evident in her poem. The influence of Romantic poetry combined with a young person's outlook on life, shows her ability to interpret and personalise knowledge. She has employed the models to create her own narrative. This is not a reproduction of 'background' knowledge, but a cultural insight into history as texts, which has found its expression in a personal voice.

The poem shows that the pupils were able to absorb rather difficult texts and turn them into models for their own personal language production. This was also the case with the other pupils' work, their diaries, personal stories and interviews with factory children. I do not think this would have been possible if we had only read texts produced for the purpose of teaching English to foreigners. Using poetry and other authentic texts from the period as source material gave the pupils access to self-expression, and enabled them to find ways of creating their own texts as expressions of self and their concepts of the foreign culture.

The material used for this project was a representation, or artefact of the way people perceived things. The learners produced their interpretations and their representations of the way the industrial revolution was perceived by others through newspaper articles, court hearings and literature. Relating personally to these texts as expressions of culture, learners gave voice to their own perceptions of the period through the characters they invented in their poems, stories and diaries. Inherent in their interpretations were their own pre-conceptions and previous knowledge. In the poem, for instance, this preconception is expressed in the final stanza where the pupil has moved the narrative into her own society and her own time. Her own preoccupations thus interact with the historical text and become part of her cultural understanding.


## Generations

This project was prompted by a chapter in the pupils' textbook. Amongst other things, the chapter dealt with the older generation. We decided to do a project about old and young people in Norway and in England. This was not only to achieve a cultural understanding about these groups in England, but also a good opportunity for the learners to gain an insight into their own grandparents' generation. It turned out that they knew very little about elderly people altogether.

First we read a chapter from Gina Davidson's *Treasure - The Trials of a Teenage Terror*. The class discussion on this text was concentrated around possible differences between being a teenager in England and in Norway, or rather, in London and in Bergen. The pupils found the text a bit complicated, but by this time most of them had developed strategies to cope with difficult authentic texts. They no longer felt they needed to understand every word, and were capable of coping with the text as a whole. The text is a humorous portrayal of the relationship between a mother and her teenage daughter, seen from the mother's point of view.

The learners thoroughly enjoyed the text. The reason for choosing this particular text, was that it gave them an opportunity to see teenage problems from the parents' point of view, and consequently regard their own teenage particularities from the view of 'the other'. The Norwegian philosopher, Jon Hellesnes expresses this understanding of self like this:

> "It is the awareness of the Other which enables me to understand and express 'my point of view', 'my body' and 'my behaviour'.... Until I have an outside, until I have a view of my own view, there exists no 'my view', no 'my inner being' or no 'my understanding of the world'."
> (Hellesnes, 1992: 90) (my translation)

Thus the 'other', whether it is a person, a text or a culture is no longer an object, but a subject with which one can interact or communicate in order to reach a better understanding of self. By finding their own problems presented in a foreign language with a sense of humour, they would hopefully see their adolescent selfishness in perspective. In the classroom discussion afterwards they found little difference between the situation described in the book and their own situation. Focusing upon the similarities between the life of an English teenager and their own lives, we could then talk about the differences. The only thing they found different was the fact that a young girl could and perhaps had to use a taxi. None of them would dream of spending money on taxis, and besides, their parents would always deliver and collect them. After this communal sharing of a piece of literature, the planning of the project was left up to the class.

They decided to make a kind of 'newspaper' to be read by everybody. They would form groups and then divide different tasks between the groups. Each group planned what type of material they wanted to collect. The material would then constitute the group's contribution to the newspaper. Here is a list of what each group decided to do:

- make a questionnaire to be answered by Norwegian pupils in three classes at their own school;
- make a similar questionnaire to be answered by English pupils of the same age-interview old people (grandparents or neighbours) and translate the interviews into English (The reason for translation was that elderly people in Norway do not necessarily speak English);
- write letters to old people in England and ask them to tell about themselves and give information about how old people in England live.

If the project proceeded according to plan, the information gathered would provide quite a lot of material for the learners to process. It was difficult to plan in detail what the next step would be, as we did not know what type of material we would obtain.

The groups making the questionnaires started their work immediately. Two sets were made, and the groups then compared the questions that they had written. They did not agree to the extent that the two questionnaires became identical, a small problem when the time came to process the material. One set of questionnaires was handed to teachers in other classes to be used during English lessons, and thus provided other learners with learning material with a real recipient in a communication process. The other set was sent off to Duchess's High School in Alnwick, Northumberland.

Some pupils wrote letters to be sent off to England. This task provided them with training in letter writing and awareness of the appropriate language when communicating with elderly people, which was different from their own personal letter writing. Because these letters were 'real' letters, they required consideration of the recipient. Awareness of the recipient is an important part of sociocultural competence, and cannot be properly understood unless the learners handle real, not simulated, communication situations. The learners in this case were dependent on the answers, and consequently had no problem in understanding that the way they presented their message would effect the result. The problem was where to send the letters. The only outlet I could think of was a few elderly people among my personal friends. As part of the task, I promised to interview a few people in England - this would provide them with some material.

The learners who interviewed members of their own families probably had the easiest job. When it came to translating, it turned out to be an important part of their cultural knowledge. They had to struggle with terminology which was old-fashioned, and forms of language they would otherwise not have encountered. Some of the interviewees came from rural areas or religious groups which provided interesting vocabulary that the pupils had to struggle with in order to convey the meaning to the reader. Interviewing grandparents became another aspect of cultural understanding. Some of the pupils had little contact with their own grandparents, and this school task provided them with an opportunity to communicate with them. In the translation that followed they had to, through an analytical approach to language, interpret the texts and thus gain a better understanding of 'the other'.

We had to wait a long time for the replies. The project was put aside while we waited for the material to be returned. Then the work resumed. The learners were left with the following material: 50 questionnaires from England and about the same amount from our own school, a long story written as a result of an interview with an 86 year old lady from Newcastle, a long letter from a former teacher from Seahouses, and some interviews with elderly Norwegian people.

The questionnaires were processed in different ways. A few of the learners were very keen on statistics and decided to make a quantitative and comparative study of the material on a computer. Others made more general comments on the answers, comparing English and Norwegian young people's habits, tastes and opinions. They divided the replies further into two categories in order to discover differences between boys and girls. Eventually the class had compiled quite an amount of material that could be used in the classroom for further study.

The task was evaluated in conversations with the various groups as they worked. This type of project entails periods of inactivity as the collection of material depends on other people's co-operation. The learners enjoyed the work, but lost contact with it when they had to wait for replies, and self-evaluation was consequently more difficult at the end.

In this project the approach to cultural understanding was more of the kind that Byram (1989) terms "anthropological" or "ethnographic" than the previous projects the class had worked on. They did not produce personal material to the same extent, but learnt a lot about collecting data and processing the information they received. It also provided the opportunity for some learners to show great skills they have achieved outside school when it came to using computers in processing data and making graphic material. At the end the material they had collected was used as a 'textbook' for all the pupils in the class.

While they had worked with this particular project, they had gained insight into the habits and opinions of groups of young people in Norway and in England, and they were in possession of material they could use for comparison. They had discovered that the greatest cultural differences were not between the English and the Norwegians, but between boys and girls, irrespective of nationality. This had rocked some of their stereotyped ideas. On the other hand they had entered into communication with an older generation and discovered that they were individuals with interesting stories to tell. The dialogue with the 'other' had hopefully enabled them to discover something about themselves and their own preconceptions.

## Conclusion

In this article I have presented two small projects on sociocultural competence carried out in a classroom of young Norwegian learners of English. I have discussed different aspects of cultural competence in each of these. The aim of both projects was to open up for insight into a foreign culture and through different levels of interaction with it, give the learners a chance to become culturally more competent. The areas of culture they ventured into were mainly defined and chosen by the learners themselves, and thus the work seemed relevant and interesting to them, although very little of the work was concerned with what textbook-writers seem to think is relevant to young people, pets, discotheques, shopping and travelling.

I believe that understanding a culture requires a dialectic approach between two subjects. In the classroom this might mean that each individual learner needs the opportunity to interrelate with the texts in order to interpret and discover his own meaning with or without the teacher's assistance. In this personal process of interpreting and negotiating meaning, the learner needs to have a qualified choice of material. I have tried to show what choice this group of learners were given.

The two projects are very different in their approaches. The former about the Industrial Revolution deals mainly with written texts which the learners read before they produce their own texts. The latter which we called Generations has an anthropological approach of questioning and gathering information which is then processed. But the projects might not be as different as they seem at first. Throughout the article I have used the term text in the widest sense, and both projects are about interacting with texts. In an article about knowledge and communication Sveinung Time sees culture like this: 'Our culture may be regarded as a linguistic landscape consisting of an infinite number of texts.' (Time 1989, 164 - my translation) A text is not an autonomous entity but a phenomenon that exists in an intertextual, communicative relationship with the reader or with other texts. It has to be interpreted and negotiated like any other communicative activity. In this way both projects can be seen as interactive discourse in order to understand the foreign text or culture, which then offers a possibility of increased understanding of self. This is Ricoeur's view : 'To believe that we reach a better understanding through introspection seems to Ricoeur a seductive illusion, we experience our own indentity through interaction with others.' (Kvalsvik, 1985: 23 - my translation) By opening up for the learners a way to gain insight into the foreign culture rather than teaching them about it, we also open up a path which might enable them to gain a better understanding of themselves.

# References

Bourdieu, P. (1993) *The Field of Cultural Production*. Oxford: Polity Press.

Bourdieu, P. (1994) *Language and Symbolic Power*. Oxford: Polity Press.

Brøgger, Fredrik Chr. (1992) *Culture, Language, Text. Culture Studies within the Study of English as a Foreign Language*. Oslo: Scandinavian University Press.

Blake, William (1970) *Songs of Innocence and of Experience*. London: Oxford UP, (1789-1794).

Brooks, P. (1992) *Reading for the Plot: Design and Intention in Narrative*. Cambridge: Harvard UP.

Brumfit, C.J. and Johnson, K. (eds.) (1979) *The Communicative Approach to Language Teaching*. Oxford: Oxford UP.

Byram, M. (1989) *Cultural Studies in Foreign Language Education*. Clevedon: Multilingual Matters.

Davidson, Gina (1993) *Treasure. The Trials of a Teenage Terror*. London: Virago.

Harrison, B. (ed.) (1990) *Culture and the Language Classroom*. ELT Documents 132. London: Modern English Publications.

Holec, H. (1981) *Autonomy and Foreign Language Learning*. Oxford: Pergamon.

Illich, I. (1979) *Deschooling Society*. Harmondsworth: Penguin.

Kvalsvik, Bjørn Nic (1985) "Forteljinga, kulturen, historia. Paul Ricoeur i samtale med Bjørn Nic. Kvalsvik". *Samtiden* 4: pp. 22-23.

Little, D. (1991) *Learner Autonomy. 1: Definitions, issues and problems*. Dublin: Authentik.

Little, D., Devitt, S., Singleton, D. (1989) *Learning Foreign Languages from Authentic Texts: Theories and Practice*. Dublin: Authentik.

Time, Sveinung (1989) "Kunnskap og kommunikasjo". In Stieg Mellin-Olsen (ed.) *Om kunnskap. Fagdidaktiske perspektiver*. Bergen Lærerhøgskole.

Unwin, R. (1988) *Questions of Evidence. Britain since 1700*. London: Hutchinson Education.

Vygotsky, L.S. (1991) *Thought and Language*. Cambridge: MIT Press.

Widdowson, H.G.(1978) *Teaching Language as Communication*. Oxford: Oxford UP.

Ziehe, T. (1993) *Kulturanalyser. Ungdom, utbildning, modernitet*. Stockholm/Stehag: Brutus Östlings Bökforlag Symposion.

# SUMMARY

## Michael BYRAM

The preceding articles arise out of specific workshops and in several cases are descriptions of particular classrooms and classes. It is one purpose of this compendium to show how the workshops have led to research, experimentation and reflection by individuals or networks, and to identify examples of good practice. Direct transfer is seldom appropriate because each situation is different. For example, the role of English in Norway makes some approaches feasible which would not be so in other countries, as Anne-Brit Fenner implies. On the other hand, case studies can be an inspiration by juxtaposing one's familiar teaching and learning situation with those described here; they start new trains of thought, encourage fresh energies in developing innovative practices.

It is also possible to see in these case studies an opportunity to reflect on the relationship of theory and practice. They often take their starting point from the theoretical proposals of a workshop animator, combining these with existing experience and the particular potential of a given situation. Now it is important to ask whether this meeting of theory and practice can in turn help to identify which aspects of theory have been useful, where there is a need for more theoretical work, what theory does not stand up to the challenge of practice. Taking this perspective, several issues become evident.

The first of these is the question of what knowledge (*savoirs*) is needed in intercultural competence. None of the articles propose a defined body of knowledge which teachers teach and learners learn. It is in the nature of their article on objectives, that Artal et al. are concerned with a comprehensive view of intercultural competence, and they state as their first objective that students should 'get near to the "minimal knowledge" shared by the community which speaks the language', but they equally imply that this is a process of acquisition and enlarging referential knowledge over time. It is therefore not the responsibility of the teacher to transmit a body of 'minimal knowledge', but rather to ensure that learners have the means of acquiring knowledge and understanding independently (*savoir-apprendre*).

The articles by Sorani and Tamponi, and by Fischer illustrate this point by emphasising that, as the former writers say, 'students can thus develop techniques and strategies they can apply independently to other aspects of English or American life and society, or of other countries and cultures.' Their article describes a specific class and topic, and the process of working with new technology, because this is part of learners' existing experience. It is however, from the teacher's viewpoint, the aim of the work to ensure that learners have transferable skills. Fischer's article focuses on classifying a number of such techniques and skills to which teachers can refer when they are planning their work with learners. It is important to note that Fischer includes techniques which challenge learners' emotional/affective response to otherness and help them to reflect upon that too, as well as acquiring skills to elicit knowledge and understanding.

The importance of involving learners in the planning is recognised by Sorani et al. and is the particular emphasis of Fenner's article. The class she describes is already familiar with an ethos of 'learning to learn', of taking responsibility for their own learning of the language. She then adds the cultural dimension and the objective of ensuring learners become interculturally competent, and experiments with two approaches. The first, 'the Industrial Revolution', was focused on written texts, whereas the second put more emphasis on what Fischer calls 'the art of questioning' and on different approaches to gathering information or data for analysis. Thus the knowledge which is acquired by Fenner's learners is meaningful to them because they chose the topics themselves. Equally and perhaps more important is what Fenner describes as 'opening up for the learners a way to gain insight into the foreign culture rather than teaching them about it', and she goes on to make the important point that the transferability of these skills can be directed not only to yet other cultures and societies but also onto learners' own.

The first point, that the teaching of knowledge and understanding of another culture and society is subordinate to the teaching of skills of discovery and analysis, is thus linked to the second: the acquisition of intercultural competence involves learners in recognising the relativity of cultural practices, values and beliefs, including their own. Sorani et al. attempted to evaluate their success in this by measuring learners' ethnocentricity. They did so in an original and interesting way, by asking learners to listen to interviews they had given before they began the work and to make their own assessment of how they had changed. Assessment and evaluation were identified as important themes in the programme of 'Language Learning for European Citizenship' and the issues with respect to cultural learning are complex and difficult to resolve. Here is therefore one of the points at which practice feeds back into theory.

The question of levels of ethnocentricity is part of the broader question which is the third issue arising from the articles: the development of new and appropriate attitudes and a readiness to engage with otherness (savoir-être). Artal et al. include 'develop positive attitudes of curiosity, open-mindedness and understanding of the cultural facts related to the target language' as one of their objectives. Fischer includes in his techniques questions to explore feelings and emotions, one's responses to otherness and difference, but also one's hopes and aspirations shared across cultural boundaries. For teachers in Western European countries, the question is often about how ethnocentricity and negative attitudes towards difference can be changed, but the presence of teachers from Central and Eastern Europe in workshops often reminded us that the problem can be reversed. Learners who have had little or no personal contact with the West, are frequently over-enthusiastic and uncritical in their understanding of other cultures and societies. In such cases, objectives and teaching and learning processes need to focus on the development of realistic and appropriate attitudes.

All of this requires pedagogical and didactic skills and knowledge on the part of the teacher. Participants in workshops are selected by their governments and are skilled teachers, teacher trainers, policy-makers, or all of these and more. It is not surprising then that innovative good practice develops between workshops, as these articles show. The inspiration of good practice may however not be enough. It needs to be combined with teacher training, as was recognised in the proposals for the programme as a whole. This is all the more important in the dimension of language teaching which we have called developing intercultural competence. Many teachers, whether trainees in initial courses or those with many years of experience, feel they have professional competence in language, and often in literary studies. They feel that they have no disciplinary basis for their work in this dimension, even though they may have acquired intercultural competence themselves.

It is for this reason that we sought articles dealing with teacher training. Nissilä describes such a course for initial trainees and demonstrates how these benefit from work which helps them to reflect upon and become more conscious of the nature of their own intercultural competence and what their responsibilities as teachers will be. He documents in detail the process involved since, as he says, 'a pre-service teacher's professional growth implies making implicit things explicit', and what is demonstrated is that the issues discussed above arising from articles about learners are also present here. Teachers are of course themselves also learners, and this does not apply only to pre-service teachers, as Mitteregger's article shows.

Even though the theme of 'la pédagogie des échanges' was not addressed until quite late in the programme, whilst this compendium was being produced, we were anxious to include work from that workshop. It demonstrates, first of all, that the growth of intercultural competence is much enhanced by actual experience of another cultural and linguistic environment. This is evident from the experience of teachers as learners, encountering new aspects of another culture, even though they have previous experience of a country where the language is spoken. They too experience the effects of juxtaposition of the other and their own, and the process of relativisation which ensues. Equally important, Mitteregger's article lays the ground for a systematic approach to teaching for exchanges, which has to be as carefully planned as any lesson for the classroom. It is encouraging to note that as a consequence of the workshop, trainers have begun to introduce the pedagogy of the exchange as a regular part of both initial and in-service courses. The Workshop itself proved to be an occasion for both intellectual and experiential learning, and to encapsulate some of the issues on which it was focused.

All planning for teaching presupposes a theory of learning, according to which teachers determine how they will facilitate learning. Their theory may be intuitive or based on research, or a combination of the two. Theories of language acquisition are well developed and useful for the language teacher, but this is not the case for the acquisition of intercultural competence. This is evident from the articles in this compendium which have little explicit reference to psychological or socio-psychological processes, except in general and intuitive terms. This is one area for further theoretical work. A second such area is that of assessment. Sorani et al. describe their approaches and by setting out objectives in detail, Artal et al. lay a foundation for assessment of learners' attainment of those objectives. In the introduction to this volume, Geneviève Zarate has suggested a framework for assessment based on a related paper produced within the overall programme (Barium and Exarate, 1994). There is however much still to do, in particular to bring good practice and theoretical work together for the benefit of both.

## Reference

Byram, M. & Zarate, G. (1994) *Definitions, Objectives and Assessment of Socio-cultural Competence* Strasbourg: Council of Europe.

# PRIORITIES AND OUTLOOK

*Geneviève ZARATE, France*

## Institutionalised mobility and intercultural competence

The concept of geographical mobility is taking on particular significance as the century draws to a close; the globalisation of exchanges and the structural transformation of conditions governing information flow are inevitably having an impact on the nature and effects of contact between cultures. Thanks to reduced medium- and long-distance transport costs, it is becoming increasingly common for people to travel to other countries. As noted by Workshop 18A, "With the progressive easing and reduction in cost of travel, an increasing proportion of pupils may expect to have the opportunity of experiencing at least one such visit or exchange in the course of their school career" (CC-LANG (96) Workshop 18A:2).

Geographical mobility is also becoming institutionalised in the education system. Distance and proximity should be mapped less on the basis of objective geographical distance than on the degree of institutionalised or non-institutionalised recognition of training courses undertaken during a stay abroad (e.g. the European Credit Transfer System [ECTS]). Institutionalised geographic mobility itself requires new skills. The general transformations are changing the nature of stays abroad, both in terms of their duration, which is becoming longer, and their aims, which are becoming more diversified. We can therefore distinguish between the following:

- short stays abroad for educational and recreational purposes (family holidays, school trips) and reasons of tourism (discovery of a country subject to constraints of time and finance);

- medium- or long-term stays related to employment (traineeship, job). These imply considerable language constraints and the requirement that the trip be cost-effective or profitable.

It is proposed, therefore, that a clear distinction be made between professional and tourist visits. The increase and transformation of geographical mobility in western societies over the past twenty years is striking: trips abroad tend to last longer, mobility is enjoyed by ever-younger age-groups, and mobility is becoming a formal part of the education system.

113

Consideration of these facts may have the following consequences for education:

- the term 'pédagogie des échanges' ("pedagogy of exchanges") refers to a sector whose specific nature is warranted;

- we propose that the objectives of study visits and school exchanges be differentiated from those of predominantly tourist trips;

- the argument of the "authenticity" of contacts made during a stay abroad is inadequate for reflection on the stay when the visit has aims other than those of tourism;

- considered from a non-tourist point of view, a stay abroad challenges views of cultural difference; in this sense, it constitutes a situation in which the intercultural aspect of language learning is predominant.

In the report "CC-LANG (96) Workshop 18A-3", the concept of "international understanding" is put forward as a basis for the educational aims of trips abroad. Among the objectives set are:

- "to create a framework in which increased understanding between young people of different nations is possible

- to increase the experience of all at every cultural level" (op. cit. 23).

Some reserve should be maintained with respect to the proposals based on a euphemistic approach to difference ("a science of friendship" 18A-3:23) where situations of direct confrontation with cultural difference are concerned. It can thus be proposed that the skills to be developed during a stay abroad should not be considered from a purely linguistic standpoint, but rather should be conducive to forms of cultural adaptability.

These situations should be considered not only as cases to be dealt with by civic education, but also as complex situations which go beyond a simplistic moral obligation, as highlighted by the following comment: "A positive experience can help to overcome ethnocentricity, avoid xenophobia, promote mutual understanding and co-operation and reinforce motivation for further language learning (...). However, an unsuccessful visit may produce culture shock and a negative effect on attitudes and motivation" (18A-2: 2). Consideration of these situations from an intercultural angle in the classroom should place particular emphasis on:

- using a single, integrated approach to preparing for the trip abroad and the return home;

- making the experience of cultural difference an opportunity to reflect on one's own national and individual identity;

- explicitly addressing, in a training situation, negative and positive images of foreign countries.

The report on Workshop 18A makes several references to the educational issues, structural difficulties and solutions found with regard to transnational co-operation. An intercultural exploration of exchange situations should make for a deeper understanding of these situations.

## Training and the intercultural dimension

One might wonder whether a multinational approach to training ("multi" denoting an indeterminate plurality) does not simply lead to ecumenism. To institute an explicit process of reflection on educational, cultural and social differences, a multinational relationship can be regarded as following a specific pattern depending on the composition of the public: training activities with a bi- or tri-national dimension do not necessarily obey the same rules. A binational relationship may lead to an approach focusing on relationships between two national contexts and a definition of their specific nature. We could speak of a bifocal view of difference in this respect. Where a relationship is at least three-way, the debate can - as a result of the very structure of the group's composition - take place within a generic and transnational approach to cultural difference.

In Workshop 15A on the initial training of language teachers, the intercultural dimension seems to be cross-disciplinary. However, although references are made to it, it is not systematically exemplified and references are disparate in relation to the overall context:

- "linguistic and cultural diversity" (op. cit.: 5).
- "attitude", 'personal development' ('savoir-faire' and 'savoir-être')" (op. cit.: 11)
- "international understanding and competence" (op. cit.: 17)
- "intercultural dimension" (op. cit.: 19)
- " 'national' or 'regional' attitudes related to customs, beliefs and prejudices" (op. cit.: 23)
- "emotional control (ethic, empathy)" (op. cit.: 37).

This profusion of terminology allows for two somewhat conflicting interpretations. On the one hand, there are sufficient references to the intercultural dimension to show a real questioning of its relevance in initial training curricula for teachers; on the other hand, their range and disparity show that this is a field which is in the process of being constituted, as illustrated by Nissilä's contribution to this volume, but is not yet sufficiently advanced to deal with existing relationships between these different conceptual issues.

To illustrate what could represent progress in teacher training, it could be proposed as an example that the following skills be required of teachers in initial training in this field:

- the ability to identify different types of disciplinary approaches to cultural difference;

- the ability to assess the teaching tools available in relation to the intercultural dimension;

- the ability to plan a visit to one of the countries of the language taught according to the aims linked to this dimension.

The following skills could be proposed as a basis for planning further training curricula:

- the ability to analyse one's own images of cultural difference with regard to the language(s) and culture(s) taught compared with languages not taught;

- the ability to design training tools with this dimension;

- the ability to analyse a medium- or long-term stay in a non-tourist situation in a country whose language one teaches.


## Conclusions

The intercultural dimension is a central concern in both workshops: it is at the core of Workshop 13, as indicated by the title "Language and Culture Awareness", and is indirectly present in Workshop 18 on "The role of educational links and exchanges in modern language teaching and learning at secondary level". It builds on other key concepts in both workshops: autonomy in the first and exchange in the second.

One workshop is devoted to a language considered of secondary status in a European context, in this case Spanish (Workshop 10 entitled "Aprendizaje y enseñanza del espagñol-lengua extranjera en la enseñanza y la educación"). The intercultural dimension is not stressed here, since the workshop deals with affirming the European language policy for a language and culture which do not play a dominant role. The concept of autonomy predominates and the multicultural dimension is not explicitly stated in the aims set out (CC-LANG (92) Taller 10: 76-77). Yet Spanish is a language which has left its mark on three centuries of Latin American culture and opens up an unusual variety of cultural contexts; it has contributed significantly, via Spanish migratory flows, to building a multicultural Europe.

But, as we have seen, most of the workshops have a conceptual interest and a range of concepts and aims which are consistent with the intercultural dimension as we propose

116

defining it. The Council of Europe must not underestimate the political importance of this dimension in a programme set up under the aegis of the Council for Cultural Co-operation, which explicitly addresses, in a common framework, the educational issues raised by the European Union and the integration of the countries of central and eastern Europe. The intercultural dimension constitutes a relevant methodological basis here.

It should be noted that the issues raised by the accession of new members to the Council of Europe have not changed the general approach of these workshops: the concept of identity has tended to be marginal in this overall approach, even if it is addressed indirectly in most of the workshops. A subsequent process of reflection focusing on the intercultural dimension should give more weight to disciplinary explorations which have been neglected: social psychology, history and geography which would give new impetus to discussions on education if they centred on issues of identity. The intercultural dimension is of particular curricular interest. Characterised by all the complexity of national cultures and histories, it calls for a multidisciplinary approach and should prove highly innovative as a result.

Reports on Council of Europe international workshops related to the theme:
(available in the language indicated by the title; 13A and 13B are a combination of English and French).

**Report on Workshop 1A.** *Curriculum development for modern languages in upper secondary, general, technical and vocational education 15/16 - 18/19.* October 1990 - Netherlands. Doc. CC-LANG (91) Workshop 1A. Compiled and edited by Gé Stoks.

**Rapport de l'Atelier 1B.** *L'élaboration des programmes de langues vivantes dans le deuxième cycle de l'enseignement secondaire général (15-19 ans)* Mars 1993 - Belgique. Doc. CC-LANG (93) Atelier 1B. Coordonné par André Baeyen.

**Relatorio del Taller 10.** *Aprendizaje y enseñanza del espagñol-lengua extranjera en la enseñanza secundaria y la educación de los adultos.* septiembre 1992 - España. Doc. CC-LANG (92) Taller 10. Compiled and edited by Emilio de Miguel Martínez.

**Report on Workshop 13A.** *Language and culture awareness in language learning/ teaching (L2 and L1) for the development of learner autonomy (age 11-18) / Sensibilisation à la langue et à la culture dans l'apprentissage/enseignement des langues (L1 et L2 et développement de l'autonomie de l'apprenant (11-18 ans)* December/décembre 1993 - Italy/Italie. Doc. CC-LANG (95) Workshop 13A/Atelier 13A. Compiled and edited by / Coordonné par Flora Palamidesi Cesaretti / Nora Galli De'Paratesi.

**Report on Workshop 13B.** *Language and culture awareness in language learning/ teaching (L2 and L1) for the development of learner autonomy* (age 11-18) / *Sensibilisation à la langue et à la culture dans l'apprentissage/enseignement des langues (L1 et L2 et développement de l'autonomie de l'apprenant (11-18 ans)* March/mars 1996 - Malta/Malte. Doc. CC-LANG (96) Workshop 13B/Atelier 13B. Compiled and edited by / Coordonné par Paul A. Attard.

**Bericht über Workshop 14.** *'Landeskunde im DaF -Unterricht für Jugendliche und Erwachsene. Regionale Vielfalt am Beispiel Österreichs'.* Mai 1994 - Österreich. Doc. CC-LANG (94) Workshop 14 - revised. Zusammengestellt von Wolfgang Hackl.

**Report on Workshop 15A.** *The initial training of modern language teachers.* June 1994 - Czech Republic. Doc. CC-LANG (94) Workshop 15A. Compiled and edited by Alena Lenochová.

**Report on Workshop 15B.** *The initial training of modern language teachers.* June/July 1996 - Poland. Doc CC-LANG (96) Workshop 15B Compiled and edited by Hanna Komorowska and Janina Hanna Zielinska.

**Report on Workshop 18A**. *The role of educational links and exchanges in modern language teaching and learning at secondary level - "Pédagogie des échanges"*. October 1995 - Norway. Doc. CC-LANG (96) Workshop 18A. Compiled and edited by Alf Olav Haugen.

These reports are available free of charge from:

Modern Languages Section,
Council of Europe,
F-67075 Strasbourg Cedex